Artificial Intelligence, Real Teaching

BIGs (Brief Instructional Guides)

Artificial Intelligence, Real Teaching: A Guide to AI in ELT
Joshua M. Paiz, Rachel Toncelli, and Ilka Kostka

Social-Emotional Learning in English Language Teaching
Luis Javier Pentón Herrera and Janine J. Darragh

Theory and Practice: Bite-Sized Activities for Teaching Reading Skills
Aviva Katzenell

Refugee Students: What Every ESL Teacher Needs to Know
Jeffra Flaitz

Genre-Based Writing: What Every ESL Teacher Needs to Know
Christine Tardy

Drama in the Language Classroom: What Every ESL Teacher Needs to Know
Carmela Romano Gillette and Deric McNish

Conflict Resolution Training for the Classroom: What Every ESL Teacher Needs to Know
Barrie J. Roberts

Teaching Vocabulary Is the Writing Teacher's Job: Why and How
Keith S. Folse

Academic Word Lists: What Every Teacher Needs to Know
Keith S. Folse

Service-Learning: What Every ESL Teacher Needs to Know
Trisha Dowling and James Perren

SLIFE: What Every Teacher Needs to Know
Andrea DeCapua

Task-Based Listening: What Every ESL Teacher Needs to Know
Steven Brown

The Three Minute Thesis in the Classroom: What Every ESL Teacher Needs to Know
Heather Boldt

Teaching Speaking Online: What Every ESL Teacher Needs to Know
Pamela Bogart

Content-Based Instruction: What Every ESL Teacher Needs to Know
Marguerite Ann Snow and Donna M. Brinton

Flipping the Classroom: What Every ESL Teacher Should Know
Robyn Brinks Lockwood

MOOCs: What Every ESL Teacher Needs to Know
Pamela Bogart

Academic Speaking and the Boundaries of Routinized Lexical Phrases
Susan M. Barone and Summer Dickinson

What Error Correction Can(not) Accomplish for Second Language Writers: Dispelling Myths, Discussing Options
Dana R. Ferris

Artificial Intelligence, Real Teaching

A GUIDE TO AI IN ELT

Joshua M. Paiz
Rachel Toncelli
Ilka Kostka

University of Michigan Press
Ann Arbor

Published in the United States of America by the
University of Michigan Press
Manufactured in the United States of America
Printed on acid-free paper

ISBN 978-0-472-03992-0 (print)
ISBN 978-0-472-22222-3 (e-book)

First published February 2025

TABLE OF CONTENTS

LIST OF FIGURES

LIST OF TABLES

ACKNOWLEDGMENTS

We would like to sincerely thank the English language teachers who have shared with us their experiences integrating AI into their teaching. Their insights, as well as their innovative teaching practices, have informed our conversations and thinking about the ideas we present in this book. As this book is a testament to the power of collaboration and exploration, we especially appreciate their willingness to support this project: Lilo Altali, Angela Petrarca DaCosta, Jamie Del Signore, Peter DiPace, Wilson Hong, Sadia Irshad, MaryLynn Patton, Balazs Szelenyi, and Brent Warner.

We would also like to thank our students. Their collaborative spirit and thoughtful contributions to class activities and discussions about AI in English language learning have inspired us to continue finding new ways to support their academic success.

Prologue

As the three of us came together to write this book, we reflected on the different ways in which we began learning about generative artificial intelligence (GenAI). For instance, Rachel recalls a casual conversation with her high school–aged son, who mentioned that his friends were using ChatGPT, and she was curious to learn more as a university instructor. Joshua recalls being initially skeptical and refraining from engaging with generative AI tools until he saw a particularly critical post from an established scholar in the field. He then decided to explore as many AI tools as possible in his roles as university-level EAP (English for Academic Purposes) practitioner, English Language teacher (ELT) teacher-educator, and computer sciences graduate student, coming to appreciate the nuanced approach needed to use them most effectively. Lastly, Ilka learned about ChatGPT while discussing an unrelated project with a colleague in early December 2022, who happened to casually ask, "Have you heard about ChatGPT?" At that time, ChatGPT had just been made available to the public, and Ilka watched how her colleague used ChatGPT to produce a paper instantaneously. Feeling worried, she wondered if her students knew about ChatGPT and wanted to learn more about it before the spring semester began. Our stories share a common thread: we were all curious, felt a sense of panic, and knew we needed to understand ChatGPT and generative AI more generally. We also sensed that these developments would cause a major disruption in education.

Due to their mutual interest in exploring GenAI for teaching, Rachel and Ilka connected in the spring 2023 semester to discuss their experiences using ChatGPT in their undergraduate and graduate English language courses. They exchanged ideas for lessons and reflections on how they went. A bit later, they learned that Joshua was also working on using AI in teaching academic English and training pre-service English language teachers. They then started talking to him about using AI to teach English. Joshua and Ilka wrote an article about common AI jargon for teachers, and Rachel and Ilka began sharing their teaching insights with audiences at professional TESOL conferences.

All these discussions and early explorations led to the inspiration for this brief instructional guide. The more we talked to our colleagues in English language teaching (ELT), the more we realized that they seemed hungry for information, guidance, and best practices as AI continued to dominate professional conversations, media, and popular press. The idea for this book came from those discussions, and as we describe in later chapters, collaboration among teachers is the most important element of experimenting with new technology and building critical AI literacy. Like the teachers we talked to, we also felt a bit daunted by the amount of information that was available, such as blogs, webinars, articles, and teaching tips for using AI. How could we keep up with all this new literature? Where would we start if we were new teachers or new AI users? We looked for a single accessible resource that brought together lesson plan ideas, current research and scholarship, and teaching tips for working with multilingual learners but could not find one. From this discussion, the idea for this brief instructional guide was born.

You might have picked up this book because you are curious about exploring generative AI applications for your own teaching and planning purposes. We recognize that many educators have mixed emotions about diving into the world of AI and trying new tools in their teaching. Whether one is an enthusiastic embracer of AI or an adamant resistor, we believe we are at a point in which we can no longer deny that AI has already disrupted education and many other disciplines and industries. As educators, our role is to engage students in learning and prepare them for meaningful English communication in our classrooms and beyond. As AI continues to be deployed in various industries, building students' critical AI literacy skills will also become increasingly necessary.

The main goal of this book is to share what we have learned so far with the hopes of helping teachers both understand and feel empowered to begin exploring AI tools. We want to share experiences from our own classrooms while helping them make sense of the issues related to AI use in ELT. For simplicity and brevity, we use the term *AI* to refer more generally to all applications that involve using large language models to mimic the kinds of tasks that humans typically do, such as "reasoning, learning, perception, prediction, planning or control" (UNESCO, 2021, p. 6). This means that our use of the term *AI* includes generative AI, constructive AI, and assistive AI, as we describe in Chapter 1.

Like other academic disciplines, the field of English language teaching is continually evolving. New pedagogical approaches enter the field and stay while others lose popularity. At the time we wrote this book, we wondered if GenAI would be another trendy topic for teachers to learn about or whether it would have a significant long-term impact on education. While AI is not necessarily new in education, the release of *generative* AI tools, like ChatGPT, Claude 2, and Gemini, has caught the attention of the mainstream public and non-ICALL (intelligent computer-assisted language learning) specialists. For instance, ChatGPT, one of the most widely known applications of GenAI, was made available to the public in November 2022. Since then, it has received significant attention and evoked a range of emotions among educators, such as excitement, fear, anxiety, and curiosity. Nonetheless, many scholars accept that AI, especially large language model–based GenAI, is likely to be seen as "one of the most disruptive technologies of our time" (Pelletier et al., 2023, p. 21).

AI, and especially GenAI, continues to develop rapidly, and by the time you read this book, it is likely that there will be applications that did not exist at the time of writing. In this book, we focus primarily on GenAI. So, as you read through these chapters, we invite you to read with an open mind and with a willingness to understand how GenAI has played and will continue to play a role in English language teaching. ELT practitioners are at a pivotal juncture, one where they are weighing the tremendous potential of GenAI-powered ELT against the nontrivial and legitimate risks that exist. Realizing the potential benefits of GenAI—such as increased personalization of learning, more effective outreach to marginalized student populations, and increased educator agency—requires addressing significant pragmatic barriers like data privacy, stakeholder skepticism, and lack of institutional and disciplinary support.

In the spirit of full transparency and given the topic of this book, we would like to be forthcoming about our own GenAI use. The three authors did not use GenAI to write any of the content of this book. The ideas that we share with readers stem from current scholarship, research we have conducted, discussions with other teachers, and our own teaching experiences. Nonetheless, we occasionally used various AI tools to reflect on their applications to our practice and to develop section titles further. Throughout the writing process, we engaged in the iterative process of exchanging ideas in numerous brainstorming sessions; providing feedback on each other's writing, revising, and rewriting; asking each other critical questions; and ensuring that we kept our audience in mind. This book is the result of these collaborations, which also reinforces our strong belief that working together to explore and understand applications of GenAI to English language teaching is crucial. We invite you to share the ideas you read about here with your colleagues both within the field of ELT and in other fields.

We also encourage you to read the chapters of this book in order because each chapter in the book builds on ideas from previous chapters. Nonetheless, we acknowledge that some readers may feel well versed in certain areas and prefer to skip to the chapter(s) they expect to be most immediately useful. Whatever your path through this book, we hope you read with an open mind and reflect on the activities and questions we have sprinkled throughout the chapters. Additionally, remember that implementing AI into instruction *never* means replacing human judgment, expertise, or teacher intuition. As you read, we encourage you to think about whether the ideas we present will apply to your unique teaching setting or serve to enhance your practice. Some activities and AI applications may address your needs more effectively than others, which is okay. Given its brevity, we hope you use our book as a complementary resource rather than a definitive guide. To facilitate this process, we have included "Make It Your Own" activities throughout the chapters to encourage reflection on and application of the ideas in the chapter, and you can use them on your own or try them with colleagues. You can also begin your foray into experimentation and AI use in whichever way you feel comfortable. As with the emergence of any new technology, completely overhauling a course or your teaching philosophy is neither advisable nor necessary because even small changes can have profound positive effects on teaching and learning.

Chapter 1

What Is AI?

"I think it [AI] has the potential to create a level playing field, but I do have concerns about the process. It's great to have AI to help with the product, but the process (critical thinking, design thinking) has to be human."

> —a project management professor of multilingual
> students at a U.S. university

With any new technological innovation comes new vocabulary for both the specialist and the layperson to understand. From floppy disks and home PCs in the late 1970s and early 1980s to social media and streaming services in the early 2010s, there have always been new tech terms that accompany tech developments (CHM, 2023). From *GenAI* and *LLMs* and *DALL-E* to *AI ethics* and *algorithmic fairness*, there is a lot of unfamiliar jargon. In this chapter, we define key terms and AI tools that exist at the time of writing, discuss how they might be used in English instruction, and explain how educators can overcome challenges.

Generative Artificial Intelligence

Generative Artificial Intelligence (GenAI) refers to applications that can create new content-such as text, images, or music-based on specific prompts from the user (Lim et al., 2023; Russel & Norvig, 2021). GenAI models are trained on large datasets of existing (human-generated) content to learn patterns, structures, and nuances from the data. When prompted, they then generate new content that is statistically coherent and aligned with their training data. Some examples include:

- ChatGPT and Google Gemini for (primarily) generating text
- DALL-E and Stable Diffusion for generating images
- Gamma App and Beautiful.ai for generating presentation slides
- GitHub Copilot and Amazon CodeWhisperer for generating code and documentation
- Amper Music and Uberduck for generating music

Constructive Artificial Intelligence

Constructive artificial intelligence, also sometimes called *corrective AI,* is a class of AI agents that does not generate novel text on its own. Instead, these tools take human-generated input and either directly modify it or provide the human user with prompts to modify or correct their initial input. With constructive AI, nothing new is generated by the agent automatically.

Perhaps the most widely known example of constructive AI is Grammarly and its subsequent releases (e.g., Grammarly Pro, Grammarly Go). AI-powered tools like Grammarly and the Microsoft Office Editor (since the 2013 release) read user-generated text and offer recommendations for how to revise it for clarity, grammaticality, and tone. Hemingway App is another example of constructive AI but one that specializes in gauging the readability of a text and making suggestions for how to create a more accessible text for different audiences. There are also constructive AI platforms for images, such as those that have come packaged with iPhone OS from Apple to edit photos, and audio-focused AI, like Krisp and Audio Audition from Adobe, that remove noise and improve overall sound quality. Constructive AI tools are perhaps the best understood by educational technology scholars and perhaps the most readily accepted by educators themselves (O'Neill & Russell, 2019; Pokrivcakova, 2019).

Assistive Artificial Intelligence

Assistive artificial intelligence (AAI) is a class of AI agents that are designed to work with other assistive technologies to enable and empower people with disabilities as they live and act on a world that has been tacitly structured almost entirely for those with "able" bodies (Edyburn, 2004). These agents include Cabot and Project Guideline, navigation AI for the blind that uses computer vision, machine learning, and AI to help them move in a safe and confident manner, or January AI to help with tracking glucose and managing diabetes care. Indeed, many generative and constructive AIs can be used in an assistive way when paired with highly specialized technologies to address the exceptionally specific needs of the individual user. Given our primary focus on English language learning, we will not discuss AAI any further.

Chatbots

A *chatbot* is a computer program that simulates conversation with human users, usually in online environments. They may also be known as conversational agents or digital assistants. Chatbots are also used to perform a variety of tasks, such as providing customer service, answering questions, and completing transactions. Chatbots typically take the form of a messaging application with space for a user to enter their query and another space for the system's response. The query and response between the user and the chatbot are often presented to the user visually as a "chat" or message sequence like many popular SMS and mobile messaging applications. However, audio chatbots also exist and are integrated into many smartphones through personal digital assistants like Siri, Alexa, and Google Assistant.

In K-12 settings, chatbots can enhance traditional English language teaching methods. For instance, a chatbot could guide younger learners through story-based scenarios where they must choose different dialogue options, helping them practice sentence construction, vocabulary, and comprehension in context. For older students, chatbots can assist with grammar exercises and reading comprehension tasks and even offer instant feedback on written assignments. Adult education, on the other hand, often requires a more flexible approach, as learners might be juggling work, family, and other commitments. Adults learning English for professional purposes could interact with chatbots that simulate business conversations, helping them practice industry-specific vocabulary and phrases. For those adults who might feel self-conscious about their language skills, chatbots offer a nonjudgmental space to practice and make mistakes, allowing for a more personalized and confidence-building learning experience.

Adaptive Learning Platforms

Adaptive learning platforms use machine learning, predictive analytics, and artificial intelligence to help educators offer differentiated instruction based on students' personal strengths, weaknesses, learning preferences, and pace through content (Kem, 2022; Cukurova et al., 2023). This technology is commonly used in foreign language instruction apps. For instance, Duolingo uses AI to adapt lessons to a user's proficiency level and recently launched generative AI-powered chatbots to provide learners with naturalistic, artificial language conversation partners (Duolingo Team, 2023). Babbel uses learning analytics to gauge a learner's projected course through the learning content and an understanding of the student's relative strengths and weaknesses throughout their time on the platform (Pelevina, 2023). Busuu, meanwhile, uses AI-backed systems to help create meaningful engagement with new lexical tokens for language learners to facilitate their uptake and acquisition (Marsden, 2019). These tools share is the ability to analyze student performance, provide feedback, and modify content delivery or task difficulty to suit each learner's unique needs.

Adaptive learning platforms have a number of possible benefits when deployed in English language teaching contexts, yet their primary strength lies in their ability to help craft individualized learning paths for students while saving teachers significant time. Additionally, these platforms can provide some feedback to learners. This near-instantaneous feedback means that learners receive reinforcement and guidance when it will be most salient to them, as opposed to a more time-displaced manner of a traditional feedback cycle. This allows the student to benefit from immediate feedback and for the educator to focus on providing more robust and accessible formative and summative feedback at key points in the learning journey. Adaptive learning platforms also allow for dynamic content adaptation, which, given the range of linguistic abilities in any given class, may be a key consideration both in keeping students motivated and invested in their learning and in enhancing accessibility to facilitate language learning and acquisition.

Intelligent Tutoring Systems

Intelligent tutoring systems (ITS), such as Cognitive Tutors, MathSpring, and iStart, are closely related to adaptive learning platforms. At a foundational level, ITSs are designed to mimic the real-time personalized guidance that a human tutor provides to address a student's unique needs (Anderson et al., 1995). One of the foundational pillars of ITSs is the student model, which maintains a dynamic profile of each learner. This model tracks a student's performance, evolves with each interaction, and captures nuances such as misconceptions, learning rates, and even potential areas of struggle. By doing so, ITSs can predict student challenges and preemptively adjust its tutoring strategies (Desmarais & Baker, 2012). This means that, unlike traditional computer-assisted learning systems that follow a linear or static curriculum, ITSs are dynamic and adaptable. They can recognize when a student has grasped a concept and move forward, or when to dig deeper into topics that need more attention. This fluid, responsive instructional approach not only personalizes learning but also aims to make it more efficient and effective. ITSs harness the advancements in AI to bridge the gap between the vast educational content available and the unique learning pathways suited to individual students (Woolf, 2009).

ITSs offer strategic solutions tailored to the needs of students learning English. In the context of English grammar, an ITS is designed to provide clear explanations of grammar rules in multiple languages (Michaud & McCoy, 2000; Roscoe et al., 2014). This multilingual approach ensures that students, regardless of their home language, have access to comprehensible resources. Additionally, the system can generate practice exercises that align with individual students' specific requirements and proficiency levels. For reading comprehension, for example, ITSs are equipped to present texts in a manner that matches the student's current language proficiency (Hielman et al., 2006; Wijekumar et al., 2013). By offering simplified versions of texts, the system ensures that the content remains accessible. After the reading activity, the ITS can deploy assessment tools, posing questions to evaluate the student's comprehension and retention of the material. Meanwhile, in writing, ITSs function as both instructional and evaluative tools (Crossley et al., 2013; Roscoe et al., 2014). They facilitate vocabulary development and grammar competencies. Moreover, they are programmed to analyze students' written outputs, providing timely and constructive feedback and focusing on areas such as structure, vocabulary usage, and grammatical accuracy. Overall, ITSs represent a sophisticated approach to addressing students' diverse and specific needs in English language acquisition.

Navigating Challenges

While the tools we describe in this chapter offer tremendous opportunities to support language learning, there are challenges that educators must remain aware of. In this section, we do not focus on the technical difficulties of any one tool; instead, we highlight five main challenges that require consideration when integrating AI into ELT.

Data Privacy and Security

The nature of AI-driven tools, especially those that utilize machine learning, requires access to vast amounts of data to function optimally. In the context of ELT, this data often comprises sensitive information about students, including their learning patterns, linguistic proficiencies, and sometimes even personal information. This kind of data could, in some jurisdictions and institutions, be considered part of their educational record and would thus be protected by law (e.g., the Federal Educational Rights and Privacy Act in the United States, *Lei Geral de Proteção de Dados* in Brazil, the Personal Data Protection Act in Singapore). In this context, then, the security of students' data and shielding its privacy becomes a non-negotiable imperative and one that not all vendors are prepared to certify. For instance, Amazon Web Services (AWS) has certified their Health Insurance Portability and Accountability (HIPAA, United States) and General Data Protection Regulation (GDPR, European Union) compliance. However, they have yet to do so when it comes to the Federal Educational Rights and Privacy Act (FERPA, United States) with their new AWS Bedrock solution (as of this writing), which provides developers with paid access to five different AI foundation models. Institutions and practitioners must, therefore, be vigilant about the data handling practices of AI tool providers, ensuring compliance with national data protection regulations and global best practices.

What can ELT practitioners do? To begin, a working understanding of both national and international data protection regulations is indispensable. By actively engaging in workshops or online courses on data privacy, educators can equip themselves with the knowledge needed to navigate this complex landscape. Prior to the adoption of any AI tool, a careful review of the AI developers' data protection policies is also crucial. This review not only ensures compliance but also offers insights into the tool's data collection, storage, and processing mechanisms. Proactive engagement with these providers and asking critical questions about their data handling practices can further highlight potential areas of concern. Institutions often have dedicated IT or legal teams versed in data privacy, so using these internal resources can provide invaluable support to instructional staff as well. By embedding these practices into their professional routines, ELT practitioners can more confidently harness the potential of AI for good while safeguarding the trust and privacy of their students.

Rapid Evolution of Tools

AI is in constant flux as tools and algorithms evolve quickly. For these reasons, a tool that is considered state-of-the-art today might become outdated in a few years or months. This rapid evolution challenges educators and institutions that have invested time, effort, and resources in integrating specific tools into their curricula. This underscores the necessity for educators and institutions to adopt a proactive approach to professional development in the realm of AI. While the technological facets of an AI tool might evolve, foundational pedagogical principles often remain consistent. As such, being aware of technological advancements is vital, yet educators should always anchor their teaching methodologies in sound ELT pedagogy. This balance ensures that irrespective of the tools in use, the quality and efficacy of instruction remain uncompromised.

Closely related to the issue of obsolescence is the lack of ongoing support. Not all AI tool providers offer consistent and long-term support for their products. Some tools, especially those developed by startups or smaller entities, might face discontinuation, leaving educators without any direction. Said another way, smaller, more specialized tools may have a much shorter lifecycle than larger, more generalist ones. This means that you may come to rely on a tool only for it to stop receiving regular updates, new features, or live customer support sooner than you would like. Therefore, it is crucial for decision-makers to factor in the longevity and support potential of a tool before its integration into the ELT ecosystem.

Gaining Stakeholder Buy-In

Many stakeholders are excited about the possibilities of AI and support teachers in their exploration of new tools. Nevertheless, new technologies and pedagogical approaches can lead to feelings of anxiety and dread. Some researchers in human-machine interaction have coined the term *AI anxiety* to help us understand how and why people may have such a visceral reaction to the emergence of AI systems (Johnson & Verdicchio, 2017; Richardson, 2015). Given the diverse array of stakeholders in ELT contexts, navigating disagreements can be a challenge all its own. Here, we turn our attention to the four main stakeholder groups with whom you may need to justify your decision to implement AI tools into your classroom practice—administrators, parents (especially in K-12 settings), colleagues, and, most importantly, students.

First, administrators may resist AI integration due to budgetary constraints and/or a lack of the technical infrastructure to adequately support the
purposeful integration of AI tools into the classroom. Additionally, they may
be resistant to change—the notion that because something has worked well
enough in the past, it remains good enough for the present and the future.
In K-12 settings, parents of young learners may worry about excessive screen
time and data privacy as their children's exposure to educational technology
increases. Fellow instructors may be concerned about being replaced by AI
systems, though early research suggests this may not be a legitimate concern
but instead one that is more grounded in the state of AI in the popular imagi-
nation because of its portrayals in media (Albanesi et al., 2023). Finally, students may resist AI in the classroom out of concerns about tech equity if they
lack stable, reliable, high-speed internet access or cannot afford subscriptions
to higher-powered models, getting "lesser" results than their peers who can
afford them. They may also worry about their privacy as they use these tools.
All these concerns must be considered and addressed through transparent
communication about AI and its potential benefits and risks to learning.

Algorithmic Fairness

Educators need to be aware of issues of *algorithmic fairness*, which often
arise because of biases inherent in the systems themselves, either because
of how they were coded (i.e., rules about the world) or because of the training
data used to build the AI model (i.e., knowledge about the world) (Mitchell,
2020; Pasquale, 2020). These biases can manifest when AI and AI-powered
tools inadvertently discriminate against certain individuals or groups by
perpetuating harmful stereotypes and assumptions. For example, a speech
recognition tool trained primarily on native English speakers may struggle
to understand non-native accents. Similarly, a text generator primed on
non-diverse data could reinforce problematic social biases by portraying
only men as doctors or women as nurses in its outputs or only producing
responses in dominant varieties of English, treating linguistic diversity as a
deficit rather than an asset.

To address these biases, instructors should vet AI tools prior to adoption
through an auditing process to assess the tool's alignment with their needs
and values. Periodic assessments should continue after they integrate tools
into their teaching. For example, they may track speech recognition accuracy
across student demographics to catch emerging issues or watch troubling

patterns in the assessments or recommendations of the system. During lessons, teachers should also sensitize students to algorithmic unfairness. For instance, the class might analyze an AI text generator's output for problematic assumptions and then compare it with equity and social justice principles. This activity connects both to the notions of critical AI literacy and educational practices aimed at developing critical thinking skills in our students.

Finally, practitioners must demand accountability from AI developers through direct engagement—vocalizing the need for continuous bias testing, transparent reporting, and improved model equity. Said another way, educators must have a voice in the room advocating for their learners. This can be realized through formalized positions on algorithmic fairness and fair and explainable AI by professional organizations (e.g., TESOL International Association, the National Council of Teachers of English, the American Council on the Teaching of Foreign Languages) and intersectional organizations like AI in Education, aiEDU, and AI For All. As Selwyn (2022) aptly states, "The use of AI in education will always be an issue of values and politics, rather than mere technical fixes" (p. 5). Prioritizing ethical integration is paramount both institutionally and individually.

Equity, Access, and Advocacy

Existing structural inequities can further complicate AI integration into English language teaching (Thomas et al., 2019; Trucano, 2023), and in some cases, it may fall upon the practitioner to navigate these complexities in part or in whole. For example, subscription and access fees to certain AI tools could be prohibitive for some students because of their economic and family realities. This is problematic because certain tools, such as custom GPTs, can only be accessed by users with a valid, paid subscription. Other times, more powerful versions of public tools are made available, or made more consistently available, to paid users. This then means that a student who pays 20 USD per month to Anthropic for their pro tier gets early access to upgraded models and is permitted to submit more queries to the system than free users, who are often limited in how many queries they can send in a three-hour period. In the case of OpenAI's ChatGPT, GPT-4 is a considerably more capable, creative, and powerful model than the freely available GPT-3.5. This means that a student who pays for GPT-4 will get better outputs than one who does not. From here, it is not difficult to see how the student who can pay for access may be at an advantage. This is to say nothing of our learners who do not even have reliable or ready access to the internet or to computer resources, relying instead almost exclusively on pay-as-you-go mobile service and smartphones. This reality can further disadvantage already marginalized groups. To take it a step further, students in rural settings may face infrastructure limitations beyond those discussed above. Finally, students with disabilities may find it difficult to use certain AI-powered tools if their user experience design has not been appropriately crafted to interface with assistive technologies on which the student may rely. Taken together, these issues represent a significant risk to student access that could exacerbate achievement gaps and further divide students along socioeconomic lines.

Make It Your Own: Navigating AI Integration

Reflection Activity: Locating AI in My Context

Reflect on your institution's stance toward integrating AI tools into ELT classrooms.

- What policies or protocols exist currently regarding AI adoption? How are teachers either empowered or restricted from using AI?
- How aware are various stakeholder groups (e.g., administrators, parents, students) of AI? Are they supportive or skeptical about AI?
- How effectively does your context prioritize equitable access when new technologies are introduced?
- What challenges might arise? (e.g., data privacy, algorithmic bias, accessibility)

Application Activity: Draft an AI Integration Proposal

1. Choose an AI-powered tool you wish to implement for language teaching. This could be an ITS, writing assistant, chatbot, etc.
2. Outline key capabilities of the tool and how it would enrich student learning experiences.
3. Address ethical dimensions like data privacy, accessibility, and bias testing.

---

4. Detail an incremental rollout plan starting with a small pilot group before wider adoption.
5. Propose strategies to foster buy-in among stakeholders by highlighting the pedagogical value of this tool.
6. Specify resources needed to promote equitable access to the tool across socioeconomic backgrounds.

After drafting this proposal, take ten minutes to self-assess if you've holistically accounted for equitable access, ethical risks, and stakeholder perspectives. Consider peer reviews from colleagues to further strengthen the proposal before submitting it to administrators. Use this exercise to reflect on proactive planning needed to integrate AI responsibly.

Chapter Takeaways

- There are a variety of AI tools which we categorize as either generative, constructive, or assistive.
- AI represents a tool for advancing human cognitive and creative abilities, but this advancement should be guided and defined by our shared human values and principles.
- Transparent communication, incremental adoption tuned to disciplinary best practices, an emphasis on equity and access, and sustained professional development are powerful ways to navigate this transformative moment.

Chapter 2
Enhancing Critical AI Literacy in ELT

"I really appreciate having a space where I can learn more about what AI *really* is and to think about what it can and cannot help me do. I really wish more professors updated their classes to make space for this kind of work."
                    —an undergraduate multilingual student in the United States

In our modern world, technology increasingly shapes our personal and professional spheres, from the rise in online relationships to the use of tablets in parenting, as noted in the popular press. This shift also extends to education, where mastering new learning management systems like Blackboard or Sakai has become essential. Reflecting on the past, skepticism around computers in classrooms, as discussed by Cuban (1993) and Papert (1987), has transformed over three decades into an acceptance and necessity of these technologies. This parallels the current emergence of AI in education, which was initially met with skepticism but now is increasingly recognized for its potential, much like the journey from writing to tech literacy.

The rise of generative AI in classrooms, which necessitates AI literacy, is a shift that is now being acknowledged, as evidenced by a bipartisan AI literacy bill in the United States (Donnelly, 2023). Unlike past transitions, we now have the advantage of rich research and perspectives to navigate this evolution from orality to literacy and now to AI literacy, provided that we remain open to embracing these changes. This chapter will explore the concept of tech literacy as an increasingly essential skill; provide a framework for critical AI literacy in English language teaching, drawing parallels from engineering and computer science education; and predict the future of AI integration in education.

New Literacies, Teaching, and Learning

If you are a language educator, you are already familiar with the concept of literacy and multiliteracies, especially as they relate to students who are navigating literate abilities in multiple languages (New London Group, 1996; Castro & Gottlieb, 2021; Watts-Taffe & Truscott, 2000), come from a background where oral traditions remain dominant, or have limited literate ability in one's first language. Thus, acquiring literacy in another language represents a particular challenge (Windle & Miller, 2012). Many of us have come to accept a more expansive approach to literacy/-ies, akin to that advanced by Brandt (1998), which sees specialized knowledge as a form of literacy such that knowledge of how to "read" a football field and understand the importance of the rituals and symbols of that community of practice represents a form of literacy.

For these reasons, a natural extension of this is the idea of *technology literacy*. Tech literacy emerged in the early 1990s in technology and engineering education before moving out into education and public life more generally (Bybee, 2000; Davies, 2011). Many earlier engineering education and teacher education scholars had varied definitions of tech literacy, ranging from the simple (i.e., knowing about technology) to the nuanced (i.e., knowing how to use technology and when and *why* to use or not use it). Because of its alignment with notions of AI literacy, we use a more nuanced definition of tech literacy, drawing heavily from the work of Davies (2011). It can be helpful to understand tech literacy as a highly emergent and evolutionary form of literacy, one that is not acquired once and then taken off the proverbial shelf when needed but one that instead continues to grow and evolve as new technologies emerge. In this sense, tech literacy represents a dynamic skill set and critical habits of mind with a shared set of end goals.

Tech Literacy

At its most foundational level, technology literacy requires one to know about technology. While not necessarily requiring deep technical knowledge of how a central processing unit (CPU) works, it instead requires the basic knowledge that modern computing devices have a CPU that handles the instruction processing and acts like the "brain" of the machine. Knowing that a computer consists of a CPU, random access memory (RAM) (like short-term/working memory), and input/output (I/O) devices (e.g., keyboard, mouse, monitor) is sufficient. However, with only basic knowledge, there is relatively little that one can do as one must understand how to use the computer to complete real-world tasks. This requires one to move beyond a simple understanding of *what* something is to a deeper understanding of *how* to use a thing. For example, this is the difference between knowing that a keyboard is needed to provide input to a computer (basic), being able to type at speed by touch with minimal error (extended), knowing how to use only a keyboard and keyboard shortcuts to completed advanced systems tasks (e.g., system administration through the command line interface) (advanced).

This knowledge also requires us to understand the *why* of implementation so that we can choose to either implement technology to support learning or remove it from the equation (Davies, 2011). Being literate to this level requires one to have enough knowledge about technology and how to use it to envision its purposeful deployment for specific purposes. Thus, knowing what a computer is does not automatically allow one to imagine possibilities for supporting learning. Applying this knowledge requires advanced tech literacy, disciplinary knowledge, and experience working in tandem to address the question of *why/why not*. Being able to do so enables one to more critically engage with technology and a tech-mediated society to make meaningful assessments of new technologies and how best to deploy them in daily life.

Despite initial misgivings, tech literacy has come to be seen as a vital part of being an engaged citizen in a modern society. For instance, community colleges, local governments, and nonprofit organizations have all taken steps to help individuals acquire basic tech literacy so that they can survive and thrive in tech-mediated workplaces as a means of moving beyond basic, lower-wage labor toward more skilled labor with better wages. However, basic tech literacy is no longer enough because of the proliferation of one key technology that is arguably an essential resource and utility in modern life: the internet.

Digital Literacy

With the proliferation of internet technologies and easy access to massive stores of information that they brought with them, a new form of literacy was needed. It was no longer enough to know what the internet was; one needed to assess, consume, and create information for a web-mediated world. This development gave rise to the notion of digital literacy, sometimes called information literacy, and it has come to be seen as an essential skill set in the modern classroom. The International Society for Technology in Education describes *digital literacy*, situated in the framework of computational thinking, as the ability to use technology to find, evaluate, create, and communicate information (Brooks-Young, 2016). As education becomes increasingly blended with web-powered technology, teachers must consider how to effectively integrate digital tools to promote student digital literacy.

Effective use of technology in the classroom requires both teacher and student digital literacy (Gretter & Yadav, 2018). Teachers must understand how to vet online resources, use digital platforms, comply with privacy policies, and teach students the cognitive and social-emotional skills to safely navigate the online world. Studies show that professional development focused on advancing teacher digital literacy leads to increased use of classroom technology and improvements in student learning outcomes (Hsu, 2016).

We believe that promoting student digital literacy begins with modeling—teachers should think aloud as they evaluate online information and demonstrate ethical technology use. Lessons can then allow students to practice critical thinking and ethical reasoning in the context of digital dilemmas, social media, online security, and identifying misinformation (Curran & Ribble, 2017). Researchers state that literacy instruction should go beyond operational, technical skills to empower students as creative, collaborative, and discerning digital citizens (Kiili et al., 2018).

With careful and intentional development of both teacher and student digital literacy skills, technology can be an asset for teaching and learning rather than a distraction. It is essential that schools continue to prioritize digital literacy instruction to prepare both educators and students to harness the educational potential of technology (Falloon, 2020). It is also important to remember that, as with tech literacy before it, one can be more or less literate, and just because someone is familiar with technology or makes ready use of it does not mean that they are inherently highly literate (i.e., the myth of the digital native). To be highly literate suggests a certain creative and critical capacity with the tool. Said another way, just because our students know where to find information does not mean they are digital literates. Indeed, many will need help to move to higher proficiency levels and to engage in critical engagement with digital information and tools, especially given the sharp rise in mis-/disinformation.

The Emergence of AI Literacy

As we have witnessed the evolution of tech literacy into digital literacy and the emergence of powerful and publicly available generative AI tools, we now see that AI literacy will be increasingly required to operate in an AI-rich world. AI literacy itself is nothing new, however, with roots in the fields of computer sciences and engineering education (e.g., Pillay et al., 2018; Tenório et al., 2023), albeit with a stronger focus on understanding the algorithms and technologies that undergird AI systems to a sufficient degree to create new AI systems and tools. Recently, however, there has been an increased call for a more generalized form of AI literacy to develop a competitive labor force (Ellingrud et al., 2023) and facilitate an informed citizenry. This more generalized AI literacy refigures the specialized form from computer sciences and engineering as its foundation—focusing on understanding AI fundamentals, learning how to use AI tools, and parsing AI-generated outputs. However, we believe that basic AI literacy skills alone will not be enough. Instead, what is needed is a more critical AI literacy that also equips individuals to parse and evaluate AI outputs and to identify the likelihood that content has been AI-generated or modified to identify potential mis-/disinformation, creating space and value around human expertise in an AI-rich world (e.g., Strauß, 2021). Here we turn to an extended discussion of what critical AI literacy entails for ELT and our continued work as practitioners working closely with English language learners.

Critical AI Literacy for ELT

Critical AI literacy can be broadly defined as the ability to understand, evaluate, and ethically use artificial intelligence, recognizing its capabilities, limitations, and societal impacts, particularly in the context of education and daily life. More specifically, critical AI literacy in the context of ELT consists of several subparts that work together to contribute to one's overall critical AI literacy, and an individual may be more competent in one area than another. Indeed, as new tools become available and the technology changes, one may find the need to "re-learn" or evolve certain AI skills and competencies. The components of critical AI literacy, which we will discuss in greater detail below, are:

1. **Understanding of the pedagogical impacts of AI systems and how to influence students' use of AI tools to support lifelong learning**

    This competency builds upon understanding how AI tools can enhance the learning process across various subjects by providing personalized learning experiences, fostering adaptive learning environments, and/or encouraging students to become active participants in their lifelong educational journey.

2. **Understanding the fundamentals of AI systems and how they operate**

> This competency pertains to comprehending the basic mechanics of AI, such as machine learning and data processing, and how these can be applied in educational settings to support diverse learning styles and needs, automate administrative tasks, and facilitate innovative teaching methodologies.

3. **Knowledge of the limits and capabilities of AI systems**

> This competency requires that educators become aware of both the strengths and limitations of AI in an educational context, recognizing where AI can supplement human instruction effectively and where it may fall short—particularly in areas requiring emotional intelligence, ethical considerations, and complex decision-making.

4. **Habits of mind necessary to use AI systems and evaluate the output of AI systems and the critical digital literacy skills to identify likely AI-generated mis-/disinformation**

> This competency involves cultivating a critical mindset in educators and students to effectively use and evaluate AI tools and outputs, along with developing digital literacy skills that are crucial in identifying and understanding the implications of AI-generated information and potential misinformation in the educational context.

5. **Knowledge of AI ethics and algorithmic fairness and how it interfaces with disciplinary best practices and theoretical underpinnings**

> This competency refers to understanding how AI ethics and fairness should be integrated into educational practices, ensuring that AI tools used in education are free from biases, respect privacy, and align with the ethical standards and educational objectives of various disciplines.

This critical AI literacy framework allows us to better think through the complexities of living and working in an increasingly AI-rich world. With new tools and technologies coming online almost daily and with students making regular use of AI tools, even if some report having a deficit view of AI because of academic dishonesty concerns, a framework can be valuable to teachers. By breaking critical AI literacy into separate parts, busy educators can more quickly assess where they need to focus their ongoing professional development. Beyond that, by identifying the areas in which they are most competent, they can connect with peers who are more proficient in specific areas, which facilitates collaboration and peer-driven professional development. To explore the framework for critical AI literacy that we propose for ELT more fully, we discuss how to gauge and grow AI literacy competencies. Here, we also rely on an example of our own assessment to highlight the need to work together to meet student needs and expectations during a time of radical change.

Gauging AI Literacy and Growing Competencies

Given the rapid emergence of technology and the speed with which new AI tools that are more capable, versatile, and available, we advocate for a collaborative approach to addressing the acquisition of critical AI literacy and its core competencies. We do, however, acknowledge that this approach can be uncomfortable and require a certain amount of vulnerability and perhaps a (perceived) threat to the professional self. However, we truly are better together, or if you prefer the sociocognitivist approach, two brains working together are often times better than one. For this reason, we extend our invitation to you to think alongside us as we dig more deeply into what critical AI literacy looks like for ELT as a field and for us as practicing educators. We will do this by embracing that call to collaboration and discussing our own experiences to reinforce our point about acquiring AI literacy. We aim to create space for all of us no matter where we are in exploring and/or integrating AI systems into practice.

Figure 1 shows the AI literacy skills introduced in the previous section placed at the vertices of a radar chart. The various dashed lines represent how well each of the authors of this book feel they have "mastered" the various competencies needed to be AI-literate. We have chosen to map our ratings to a radar (or spider) chart to allow you to see the "shape" of our literacy more quickly and to see where our strengths and weaknesses lie. Immediately, you should notice a couple of peculiarities.

First, you may notice that none of us have a perfect pentagon shape to our AI literacy, nor do any one of us have all our marks at the five, or "expert," rating. Indeed, from this chart, we could best describe ourselves as "highly skilled early adopters" (Rachel and Ilka) and "expert power users" (Joshua,

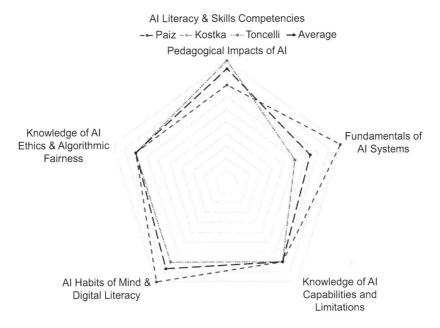

Figure 1 Comparative Radar Chart of AI Literacy and Skills Competencies

due to greater technical understanding). The second element you may notice is that we tend to balance each other out, with one author's growth area being another's strengths. The exception to this appears to be in the area of AI ethics and algorithmic fairness, which is itself a relatively new subfield of inquiry in AI, ethics, and computer science. Finally, you will likely note that it is relatively easy to identify the parts of the graph for one author (Joshua) and the average of the group but that there seems to be only three sets of lines instead of four. This is because the assessment scores for Rachel and Ilka were the same in each category.

As nice as a radar chart may be at presenting differences in the characteristics of two or more groups, there is a little bit of nuance lost in relying solely on data visualization. Thus, we return to the text to drill into this more deeply and explore the proposed critical AI literacy framework more fully. Here you may notice subtle shifts in tone and voice as each author offers some of their unique insights. We will, however, return to the organization of the framework to help carry the discussion in this section forward.

Pedagogical Impacts of AI on ELT

We have chosen to front-load this competency due to the nature of our work as ELT practitioners, teacher educators, and scholars. We see a critical role for generative AI in providing more individualized learning, automating certain administrative tasks, and empowering students to become lifelong learners by scaffolding their agency over the learning process. Perhaps most importantly, this also means knowing now just which AI systems to deploy for which tasks—for example, knowing to use something like Claude 2 when greater information fidelity is required and using ResearchRabbit when exploring a domain of knowledge and the history of scholarly conversation—but may also include possessing the judgment needed to know when *not* to use AI tools.

For Joshua, it was tempting to mark himself higher, as his current roles are classroom-focused, but he admittedly spends more time learning about the technical side of AI because of his work in the field of computer science and application development. As such, he spends some days thinking more about code and coding than pedagogy and teaching. For Rachel, this competency felt like her strength because it is most related to her existing expertise. Considering the pedagogical impacts of AI felt like an extension of her understanding of the learning process rather than something entirely new. Lastly, Ilka became interested in exploring applications of generative AI primarily because of her role as an educator. She knew that students were already using ChatGPT soon after its release and wanted to learn more about it in order to teach and support them more effectively. The three authors agree that prioritizing educational uses of generative AI requires an individual to grow their competency in identifying and utilizing AI tools as a resource to empower both teachers and learners in educational settings.

At its core, however, this competency will likely become critical to the work of ELT practitioners in an increasingly AI-rich world. This is why it was prioritized in our proposed critical AI literacy framework even though it is reliant on other, more foundational competencies, such as understanding AI systems and their limits and capabilities. Indeed, an understanding of AI's potential pedagogical implications can not only help prepare educators to be adaptable in their teaching practices but also better connect them with students to carry out the very human labor of education.

Understanding the Fundamentals of AI Systems and How They Operate

Here we want to stress that you do not need a deep technical understanding of AI systems and how they work. For example, you do not need a profound understanding of the math behind gradient descent or the ability to carry out operations on tensors on the back of a napkin. If reading that made you want to momentarily dissociate, do not worry. For the ELT practitioner, this competency is more about understanding applicable metaphors for AI (e.g., it is not like a library of information but more of a research assistant working *in* a library). It is more about understanding that modern AI systems engage in a form of *learning* about the world around them based on the *training data* to which they are exposed, often using a mix of *supervised* and *unsupervised machine learning*, along with a basic knowledge of what these terms refer to. You *do not* need a doctorate in engineering in AI to possess some form of AI literacy, just as you do not need a doctorate in philosophy or education to possess most forms of (more traditional) literacy.

For Joshua, much of his professional energies have been focused on taking an interdisciplinary approach to understanding AI systems and their underlying technologies (e.g., machine learning, natural language processing, deep learning), which is driven largely by a push to improve his skills in data and computer science during the early days of the pandemic. Given this fact and that the great amount of time he spends consuming computer science journals (and journalism) and active membership in organizations like the Association for Computing Machinery and the IEEE Education Society, he marked himself very highly here. He even teaches these fundamentals to students in his EAP and college composition courses. For Rachel, this competency has felt like the newest terrain. Since ChatGPT appeared on her radar in late 2022, she has been reading, exploring, and collaborating with peers to deepen her knowledge, yet she recognizes that her competency is still emerging. Similarly, Ilka finds many of the popular AI tools user-friendly (e.g., Twee, ChatGPT); however, she is still experimenting with these tools and learning the nuances of how they work.

Despite being second on our list, we see competency in this area as foundational to all others. One must understand the very basics of how AI works to proactively and meaningfully use them. Just as knowledge of mobile computing (e.g., using your smartphone) rose in importance through the 2010s, knowledge about AI will become increasingly important through the 2020s and beyond. Said another way, knowing about AI means knowing that you can now pay for access to the underlying *foundation models* of AI, like Anthropic's Claude (through AWS Bedrock) or Google's Gemini (through Google Cloud AI). This then means that if an educator takes a critical look at a new tool, they will know to question which foundation model is being used to determine whether it is an accurate and trustworthy tool, something that truly offers unique functionality or merely a different use of an existing tool that they might already be paying for.

Knowledge of the Limits and Capabilities of AI Systems

This competency refers to one's ability to recognize when and how AI tools might supplement human action and expertise and where they might not meet our needs. For example, a student in one of Joshua's TESOL Institute classes once quipped that AI was useless because it could not finish a sentence from his unpublished novel when he put in the first three words of the sentence. The student thus concluded that AI was not worth talking about for educators. Many of us have seen the AI hype engine at work, as proponents have promised that AI will be our best friend, outperform us on affective tasks, or be indistinguishable from a human on the telephone. In both cases, someone with some competency in this area would see that what we have is a student who does not understand the capabilities of the AI tool they were using. The platform the student used was *not* designed to finish text from an unpublished manuscript with 100 percent fidelity and had no contextual prompting about *what* the user was looking for from the system. In the other case, we would know enough to say the claim that an AI phone agent can be indistinguishable from human beings on the phone is still rather far off because of processing delays and imperfect prosodic features in the audio output that do not match natural speech.

For Joshua, he critically marked himself lower here. While he feels well aware of AI's limitations, he sometimes feels that his ability to counter those limitations is emergent, especially given the speed with which even established tools like ChatGPT or Google Gemini are changing. Additionally, most of his work with students in this area has focused on awareness-raising instead of active mitigation strategies. Rachel also marked herself critically here as she shares a sense of awareness of limitations but is still actively developing skills to address those limitations on both front-end and back-end uses of AI. Finally, Ilka marked a lower score here given the many unknowns that remain as generative AI continues to develop. Because she also continues to experiment with new tools, she feels that her knowledge in this area is still emerging.

For the ELT practitioner, competency in this area is necessary not only to join in (inter)disciplinary conversations about AI or to evaluate new AI tools that you or your students may be using. Indeed, it is also important for assessing potential AI outputs and identifying when additional attention may be needed to identify AI-generated mis-/disinformation.

Habits of Mind and Critical Digital Literacy

The phrase *habits of mind* refers to the ways in which individuals deploy their skills and knowledge to engage in meaningful, purposeful, and appropriate action. This competency focuses on the habits of mind necessary to engage with AI content and to use AI tools. It includes but is not limited to capabilities like flexibility and curiosity in exploring new tools and potential use cases; critical thinking to discern the influence of AI on a text, image, or video; engaging in continuous learning; reflective practice; and problem-solving with AI tools. More than this, however, is building advanced digital literacy skills so one can become more proficient at identifying possible AI outputs and potential mis-/disinformation and understanding the implications of AI-generated content on teaching, learning, and living in an AI-rich world.

For example, this competency for Joshua has taken the shape of engaging with AI systems as a teacher, a teacher educator, and a student, noting the different ways in which AI tools like Claude or Gamma App are used for different purposes and how prompting and dialogue change when working from each of these roles. He has found this a particularly helpful approach in considering how he talks about AI with his students, whether they are future ELT practitioners or international students in academic literacy classes. For Rachel, fostering habits of mind and critical digital literacy is an ongoing and open process of experimentation and reflection alongside teaching colleagues, in-service teachers she consults with, and students. Lastly, Ilka sees a direct link between her experimentation with AI tools in teaching and the professional development activities she has engaged in to build her own AI literacy skills. Thus, cultivating a habit of mind about AI involves a natural interplay between what she reads and learns about and how she uses those tools in class and outside of class to support teaching.

We feel quite strongly that competency in this area will be critical not only for educators but also for many going forward. We have already seen the very real personal and social damage done by mis-/disinformation *before* the emergence of powerful generative AI tools. Given this fact, explicit training for both teachers and students is necessary at all levels. Indeed, when we read stories of AI paragons warning of AI's threat to humanity, we (the authors) are far less worried about AI robots run amok, the efforts of companies like Palantir notwithstanding. We are far more worried about AI-generated mis-/disinformation and its impacts on social order and stability.

Knowledge of AI Ethics and Algorithmic Fairness

AI ethics is a relatively new area of scholarly inquiry in computer science, and one of the first truly interdisciplinary efforts in AI, bringing together linguists, sociologists, psychologists, ethicists, computer scientists, and philosophers, among others. Broadly speaking, AI ethics deals with the responsible creation and use of artificial intelligence, ensuring that AI systems are developed and operated in a way that is fair and transparent, respects privacy, and does not harm individuals or society. AI ethics also involves considering the moral implications and societal impacts of AI, including issues of bias, accountability, and the rights of those affected by AI decisions. This often requires an awareness and understanding of *algorithmic fairness*, the knowledge that as AI systems learn about the world, they often acquire many of the biases that already exist in society, further reifying them and potentially amplifying their effects.

For Joshua, gaining competency in this area has involved engaging with the accessible literature that exists through popular press sources written by AI scholars with backgrounds in sociology, law, philosophy, and the letters (e.g., Christian, 2020; Crawford, 2021; Pasquale, 2020). From there, he began to consider how he could revise class activities about critical thinking to also address thinking about the AI tools we might use in class. For Rachel, turning to literature has also been effective, and she continues to enhance her competency in this area by attending interdisciplinary webinars and conferences. Because AI impacts all professional spheres beyond education, thinking more broadly with others has been useful. Ilka recognizes that this is a growth area for her skill set, having less experience with philosophy, ethics, and legal studies. Thinking critically about her emerging competency in this area has motivated her to explore scholarship in this area and begin drawing parallels to English language teaching.

Given that multilingual students may be the most at risk as AI tools are deployed to greater effect in educational settings, we would argue that

AI ethics and algorithmic fairness will come to define many of our disciplinary conversations after we address more immediate pedagogical questions. We will need to grapple with the ethics of AI tools assessing our learners—either in the classroom or once they enter the labor market—and the implications of AI systems potentially preferring racialized, prestige varieties of English and ways of presenting knowledge over others.

A framework can provide us with a means of making sometimes complex and "fuzzy" concepts more familiar. Additionally, it can provide us with a shared vocabulary to engage in discussions with our peers about the opportunities and challenges facing us in the classroom and as a discipline. Beyond that, it can help reduce anxieties by providing an accessible entry point and removing some of the unknown. We will discuss one road map to help you conceptualize your journey to greater AI literacy and, where appropriate, integration with your practice and teaching philosophy. First, however, we encourage you to take a moment to reflect using the "Make It Your Own" activity below.

Make It Your Own

Application Activity

1. **Reflective Self-Assessment:** Begin by reflecting on your current understanding and application of each of these areas in your educational practices. Consider your experiences, challenges, and successes related to each competency in the critical AI literacy framework discussed in this chapter.
2. **Self-Assessment Scale Explanation**
   - **0—No Awareness:** You have no awareness or understanding of this competency, having heard of it only upon reading this chapter.
   - **1—Basic Awareness:** You have heard of it but lack detailed knowledge and practical experience.
   - **2—Developing Understanding:** You have a beginning understanding of the competency and/or are developing practical application skills.

- **3—Competent:** You possess a solid understanding and/ or have practical experience or application in this area and maybe have had guiding conversations with peers.
- **4—Proficient:** You have a strong understanding and significant experience; you can apply this knowledge effectively in teaching and learning and/or you're contributing to initiatives in this area.
- **5—Expert:** You have an in-depth understanding and extensive experience; you are capable of teaching others and/or leading initiatives in this area.

3. **Self-Evaluation Criteria:** For each area, ask yourself the following questions:
   - How familiar am I with the concepts and theories underlying this area?
   - Have I applied these concepts in a practical educational setting?
   - Can I effectively communicate and explain these ideas to others?
   - Am I aware of the latest developments and research in this field?
   - How confidently can I handle challenges related to this area?

4. **My AI Literacy Radar Chart:** Once you have taken a moment to self-assess, plot out your own AI literacy radar chart to see the shape of your current critical AI literacy levels. We would encourage you to make a copy or use pencil and return to this activity after a few months of continued professional development to see how your learning may have changed over time (Figure 2).

5. **Honesty and Openness:** Approach the assessment with honesty and openness. Acknowledge areas where improvement is needed since this is a tool for personal and professional growth.

6. **Plan for Improvement:** Based on your assessment, create a plan for improving areas where your knowledge or skills are weaker. This might include professional development courses, workshops, reading, or practical experimentation.

One challenge of acquiring critical AI literacy and then applying new competencies and habits of mind to implementation is feeling lost. Lost in the dense fog of technical descriptions. Lost in the forest of new tools. Lost in the winding and clogged roadways that are the rapidly expanding (inter-)disciplinary conversations on AI. These are all legitimate issues, some of which can speak

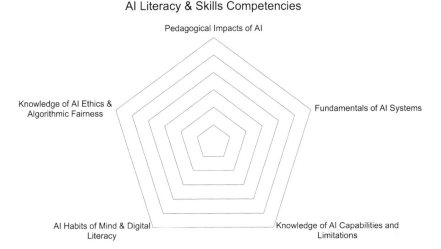

Figure 2 Framework of AI Literacy and Skills Competencies

to the challenges brought on by times of rapid, disruptive change, and some of which can speak to the challenges of facing an uncertain future. It is not our place to question any of the anxieties that you may be feeling. Instead, our goal is to equip you with tools that can help lessen that feeling of being lost, overwhelmed, or anxious.

To that end, we suggest adopting the metaphor of the road map, commonly used in project management and agile software development. A road map, in this context, gives us a simplified view of the journey ahead of us. It may contain:

- A destination
- A path forward
- A set of milestones to reach

The road map we display in Figure 3 consists of five key milestones that we hope will help you gauge your progress and ease some anxiety. Before we explain the details of the road map, we encourage you to bear two important facts in mind. First, while the road map as a visual metaphor tends to move into a rather linear representation, this journey is far from linear and has no clear end point. This is in no small part because of how rapidly the AI in education landscape is changing and newer, speedier, and more capable models become available and as existing tools may get scaled down to run locally on our smartphones and computers. We would like to emphasize that you are

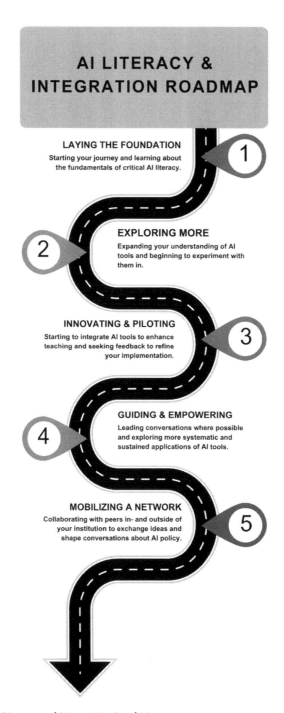

Figure 3 AI Literacy and Integration Road Map

not on this journey alone. While we have been pleased to be on this part of the journey with you, we encourage you to view this journey as a highly collaborative one at all stages and actively seek opportunities to work together with others in your institution or department to ease cognitive and affective burdens.

To give you a general sense of the road map and to create space for you to make it your own, we look very briefly at the five major stages identified in it. Remember that we encourage you to view this iteratively and collaboratively as you localize this road map to your own journey.

Laying the Foundation

This inaugural milestone encourages you to begin your AI literacy and integration journey by having an on-ramp where you can catch up to speed with your fellow travelers. In this case, it involves acquiring the foundational knowledge about AI systems that we discussed earlier (i.e., understanding that neural networks exist, that large language models drive many of the powerful generative AI tools on the market today, and that bias and fairness are legitimate concerns that we should be working to ameliorate). To help you move through this milestone, we encourage you to continue reading about AI in language education and participate in both disciplinary (e.g., TESOL International), industry (e.g., Grammarly), and interdisciplinary (e.g., IEEE Education Society) webinars and conferences to build your knowledge base and to raise your awareness of the available tools and their capabilities and limitations.

Exploring More

At this milestone, you are beginning to take those initial steps to seeing how AI tools might align with your teaching philosophy and practice. You may also begin to expand your knowledge base with a more nuanced understanding of AI fundamentals through workshops with organizations like AI for Education, AIEdu, and DeepLearning.AI. Here, you are "trying on" ideas and engaging in a form of directed play to see what works for you (and your learners) and what does not. Here, you also begin to separate the useful information and tools from considerable AI Hype.

Innovating and Piloting

When you reach the innovating and piloting milestone, you begin to take a more systematic approach to deploying AI literacy and tools into your educational practice and may even begin to use AI tools in a limited capacity *with* your students. While traveling through this marker, we encourage you to collaborate both with your peers and with your students, seeking to gain insights to refine your implementation of AI into your practice to better meet real learners' needs and align with disciplinary best practices.

Guiding and Empowering

You begin to use your emerging expertise and experience to engage in conversations and to empower your learners and your peers on their own AI literacy journeys. This may include a more systematic approach to deploying AI tools with feedback from students and an analysis of that feedback to drive the revision of lessons or materials. It may also mean partnering with a colleague to start leading workshops in your institution or regional professional organizations and guide the conversation on AI literacy and integration.

Mobilizing a Network

It is true that modern problems are interdisciplinary problems. Even the insular field of computer science has had to come to grips with the fact that many modern research questions about artificial intelligence and machine learning can only be answered by an interdisciplinary team working together and learning from each other's diverse perspectives. At this milestone, you begin to mobilize your network, such as people you have met at conferences or for coffee or as part of your online professional learning network (PLN). In this stage, you begin to collaborate on devising new pedagogical approaches to AI in ELT, exchange ideas, and shape conversations about AI policy.

Make It Your Own

Application Activities

To help you visualize and plan your journey through the five stages of AI literacy and integration, creating a personalized road map can reflect your current position and goals as well as the steps you need to take to advance.

1. **Self-Reflection and Assessment:** Start by reflecting on your current understanding and experience with AI in education. Use a scale from 0 (no awareness) to 5 (expert) to rate yourself on key aspects such as understanding of AI concepts, practical experience, ability to communicate AI ideas, awareness of latest developments, and confidence in handling challenges in AI.
2. **Creating Your Personal Road Map**
   - **Drawing the Road Map:** On a blank sheet of paper, draw a road map. Label the start, the five major milestones as discussed in the book (Laying the Foundation, Exploring More, Innovating and Piloting, Guiding and Empowering, Mobilizing a Network), and the end point.
   - **Plotting Your Position:** Based on your self-assessment, mark your current position on the road map.
   - **Path Planning:** For each milestone ahead of your current position, write down specific actions or steps you need to take to reach that milestone. These can include reading certain materials, attending workshops, trying out AI tools, or collaborating with others.
3. **Setting Milestones and Goals:** Under each milestone, write down what achieving that milestone would look like for you. This might include specific skills acquired, projects completed, or feedback received.
4. **Reflection and Adjustment:** Reflect on the road map and consider if it aligns with your personal and professional goals in AI literacy and integration. Adjust your road map as needed.
5. **Review and Revise Periodically:** Keep this road map accessible and review it periodically (e.g., every three months). Update it as you progress, reflect on your journey, and adjust your goals and actions.

Chapter Takeaways

- From the early days of computers in the classroom to the emergence of the internet, we have experienced tremendous changes involving technology and learning.
- Literacy provides a powerful framework for thinking and acting in an AI-rich world; in this case, we proposed a critical AI literacy framework.
- Viewing AI literacy acquisition and implementation as a journey allows us flexibility and grace as we navigate these changing and sometimes challenging roads together.

Chapter 3
AI on the Back End: Supporting Planning, Materials Development, and More

"In the past, material preparation could take a lot of time. Even though teachers had very good teaching ideas, they may not implement them owing to time constraints. Now teachers can dedicate more time on designing and conceptualising lessons, and outsource certain repetitive/time-consuming preparation tasks to AI."
— an English language lecturer in Macao, China

In the next two chapters, we adopt a computer science metaphor to conceptualize teaching in the AI era, viewing it through a front-end and a back-end lens. The *front end* represents the direct, student-facing aspect of teaching, akin to an app's user interface. Conversely, the *back end* involves the unseen but essential planning and professional development, similar to software's coding. This metaphor captures the multifaceted nature of teaching and emphasizes the integration of both aspects for effective learning. In this chapter, we focus on the back end because despite the shared goals among English language teachers in diverse global contexts, they face similar challenges such as teaching varied proficiency levels and institutional constraints (Ray, 2013).

AI in Lesson Planning and Assessment

Crafting effective lesson plans demands a considerable amount of teachers' time as it requires intentional *interleaving*. Interleaving "involves two related activities that promote high levels of long-term retention: (a) spacing out learning sessions over time; and (b) mixing up your practice of skills you are seeking to develop" (Lang, 2016, p. 65). For the English language teacher, this process requires cycling through short- and long-term language objectives and connecting new and previously studied material. When it comes to interleaving, we see AI as an invaluable lesson-planning assistant.

As a lesson-planning assistant, AI can do more than just help us map regular interleaving into our lessons. It can also help us think about how lesson plan considerations fit into broader curricular goals. Table 1 shows possible AI supports for these considerations, including more efficient standards-aligned planning, detailed consideration of both content and language objectives, and planning for a variety of proficiency levels.

We have been exploring how AI-powered tools can be leveraged to support lesson planning and broader curricular goals, finding that AI can save us time and mental energy and allow us to engage with students purposefully in support of their academic goals. For example, we have utilized generative AI to design creative role-playing exercises, develop dialogues that incorporate certain target sounds and pronunciation patterns, and generate written

Table 1 Overview of AI Supports to Consider How Lesson Plans Fit into Broader Curricular Goals

General Considerations	Possible AI Supports
Opportunities for interleaving and scaffolding	• recommend optimal sequences for interleaving concepts to improve retention and understanding • generate materials that incorporate previous learning alongside new learning • suggest ongoing scaffolding strategies for a variety of proficiency levels
Standards-based instruction	• align lesson plans with specific content and language educational standards • align lesson plans to align with local/national/international educational standards (e.g., CEFR, etc.).
Content and language objectives	• analyze content to suggest appropriate language objectives for lesson plans • translate content to help address language diversity in the classroom as a tool for cross-linguistic analysis • identify cognates across the languages of the classroom • design activities and materials that target specific language structures or pragmatic interactions
Proficiency levels	• adjust language for accessibility to language proficiency • map language structures and academic vocabulary that may need additional scaffolding or explicit teaching • generate scaffolded materials and activities and/or personalized learning paths based on students' proficiency levels

models for students to analyze. Table 2 lists some of the many considerations in lesson planning, as well as the strategies through which AI-powered tools can support teachers.

We have also used ChatGPT and other AI tools to help us analyze content. From these starting analyses, we have generated lesson plans, images, and slideshows for use in our classes. To do this, we have utilized iterative *prompt engineering*, which is the practice of crafting and refining carefully structured queries to guide AI tools toward precise and desired outputs. In each of these examples, we recognize that our pedagogical knowledge as ELT professionals has been essential to smart prompt engineering and to critically evaluating and adapting AI-generated materials. Using tools in this way also offers teachers insight into ways to meet the needs of all students. For example, AI can help teachers apply universal design principles to an assignment prompt or announcement to increase accessibility for students. While this sounds like a monumental task, it does not require them to engage in months of trial and error. In harnessing the power of AI, they suddenly have a teaching assistant to offload time-consuming background work, freeing them to focus on teaching.

AI tools have also helped us identify target academic vocabulary from a reading, as well as cognates and key language structures that are essential to comprehension. For example, when one of the authors collaborated with a group of middle school science teachers who were struggling to make content accessible to their multilingual learners, she prompted ChatGPT to identify academic vocabulary and cognates and to generate leveled versions of the reading and comprehension questions. Below we list some of the prompts used to explore how best to teach content while also building upon varying proficiency levels.

1. [Input copy of text students will be reading] This reading is for a group of sixth-grade students whose home languages are English, Spanish, and Portuguese. Use this reading to respond to subsequent questions.
2. Generate a list of the academic vocabulary required to understand the reading and provide a definition for each word/phrase.
3. Generate a table with four columns. The first column should include the academic vocabulary in English; the second column should include the definition in English; the third column should include a cognate in Spanish, if there is one; and the fourth column should include a cognate in Portuguese, if there is one.

Table 2 Overview of AI Supports of Lesson Plan Detail

Detailed Lesson Planning Considerations	Possible AI Supports
Translanguaging opportunities for home languages	• generate cognates and/or text translations for metalinguistic analysis • develop classroom vocabulary labels in multiple languages • revise materials to be more inclusive of non-Western varieties of English
Creating connections to lived experience and prior learning	• suggest warm-up activities based on students' interests and background • offer insights into student interests and experiences through data analysis, aiding in creating relevant connections • suggest activities that create cyclical interleaving of content to connect new learning to prior learning
Frontloading academic vocabulary	• determine academic vocabulary for given reading/content areas • generate activities relating to building this vocabulary (e.g., interactive games, finding collocations) • generate images relating to the vocabulary or theme for discussion and vocabulary reinforcement • provide pronunciation models
Creating content – delivery, materials	• recommend appropriate teaching materials and delivery methods based on content and learning objectives • create interactive content and multimedia materials to enhance engagement and understanding (e.g., video, activities, role-playing exercises, comprehension/discussion questions, etc.) • curate videos with comprehension and/or extension questions • develop slides and images • create models for student analysis (e.g., sample paragraphs, essays, etc.) • revise materials to better connect with neurodiverse and culturally diverse learners

Detailed Lesson Planning Considerations	Possible AI Supports
Providing multimodal access	• create content in various formats (e.g., text, audio, video, images) • provide transcriptions of audio content • create images relating to content or vocabulary for discussion and review • create dialogues to practice particular sounds, structures, or vocabulary
Neurodivergent inclusion	• tailor instructional strategies to support neurodivergent students, adapting content and delivery methods to suit unique learning needs • support universal design of learning to create lessons that are accessible to all learners • utilize speech recognition via assistive AI
Equitable access to content (for MLL teachers that provide support via push-in to content areas)	• create adaptive content that caters to different linguistic proficiency levels within the same lesson • modify linguistic content to match varying levels of complexity, ensuring that all students can engage with the material (e.g., adjusting the language of word problems or making primary sources in history more accessible) • design linguistic scaffolds/classroom activities to make content comprehensible while also supporting emerging language skills
Lesson plan feedback	• review existing lesson plans for accessibility through a variety of lenses (e.g., avenues to access home language and/or prior knowledge, appropriate scaffolds for varying proficiency levels, opportunities for student agency, etc.) • evaluate lesson plans and related materials to ensure intersectional representation and equitable access to language and content

4. What are the most important grammatical structures that a bilingual student needs to comprehend the original reading in English?
5. Adapt the original reading for speakers with a lower proficiency level in English.
6. Create five comprehension questions on main ideas for students with high proficiency in the English language and a second set for lower-proficiency students. Each set of questions should cover the same main topics, but the second set should be more accessible linguistically.

Common advice for utilizing AI for lesson planning includes developing good prompt engineering skills. Indeed, a twenty-first-century skill that educators will need is the ability to purposefully prompt LLMs to maximize their power to assist us with customizable and flexible instructional plans and materials. (See Chapter 7 for prompting guides.) Initial prompts, though they may include context, content, and task, often do not immediately generate ideal output and often require additional prompting. Table 3 shows an example of how a generic prompt can be customized to improve the quality of the output.

In our work supporting pre-service and in-service teachers, we often refer to the computer science concept of GIGO, or "garbage in, garbage out," which recognizes that the quality of output is directly related to the quality of input. Cain (2023) suggests that prompt engineering "mirrors many principles from design thinking, where [it] starts with a vision, undergoes planning, design, testing, and subsequent refinement" (p. 4). Through this process of iterative refinement, ELT practitioners can make the best use of AI tools to personalize teaching to their particular students and community and align teaching to specific learning goals.

Table 3 Example of Precise Prompting to Improve Output

Generic Prompt	Improved and More Precise Prompt
Generate a lesson plan to practice the simple past in English.	Generate a 90-minute lesson plan to practice the irregular forms of the simple past in English. My students are in high school with intermediate English proficiency. Their home languages are Spanish and Portuguese. Include detailed interactive activities that utilize words that are cognate between English, Spanish, and Portuguese. Include suggestions for formative assessment at the end of class.

Make It Your Own

Reflection Activity

Consider a recent lesson plan you have developed or implemented. Now, imagine incorporating an AI-powered tool to enhance some aspect of that lesson (e.g., student engagement, personalized learning, or assessment).

- What AI tool would you choose, and why?
- How would you integrate it into your existing lesson?
- What potential benefits and challenges might arise from using this tool?
- How could the use of AI align with your teaching philosophy and goals?

Take fifteen minutes to jot down your thoughts or sketch out a revised lesson plan incorporating the AI tool. Then reflect on how this exercise might change your approach to lesson planning in the future.

Application Exercise

AI Lesson Planning Feedback

AI can be a powerful tool to use behind the scenes to help manage the prep work that goes into delivering great educational experiences for students. To that end, the activity below seeks to demonstrate this potential. You're welcome to use the GenAI of your choice.

1. **Choose a Lesson Plan:** Select a recent lesson plan you have developed or implemented that you would like to receive feedback on.
2. **Select an AI-Powered Tool:** Identify an AI-powered tool that is capable of providing feedback on lesson planning. This could be a text analysis tool, an educational AI platform, or even an AI writing assistant like OpenAI's models.

3. **Prepare Your Prompt:** Use the following template to craft a prompt for the AI:
   - "I have a lesson plan focusing on [describe the key elements of the lesson, such as topic, objectives, activities, and assessment] for [describe students age and proficiency levels]. Could you provide feedback on its coherence, relevance to the target audience, and any suggestions for improvement?"

4. **Submit Your Prompt:** Enter your prompt into the selected AI tool.

5. **Analyze the Feedback:** Carefully review the AI's feedback. Consider the following follow-up questions to ask the AI or reflect on:
   - "Can you elaborate on the suggestion about [specific aspect]?"
   - "How might I improve the [specific activity/assessment/other component] in this lesson plan?"
   - "Are there any additional resources or techniques that could enhance this lesson?"

6. **Reflect on the Experience:** Take fifteen minutes to jot down your thoughts on the process. Think about:
   - How did the AI's feedback align with your teaching philosophy and goals?
   - What potential benefits and challenges did you encounter in using this AI tool?
   - How might you integrate AI feedback into your regular lesson planning process in the future?

7. **Optional—Revised Lesson Plan:** If you found the feedback helpful, sketch out a revised lesson plan incorporating the AI's suggestions. Consider sharing this with a colleague or supervisor for further feedback.

Note: AI feedback is a tool and does not replace human judgment and expertise. Always consider the feedback in the context of your own knowledge of your students, curriculum, and teaching context. Use it as a complementary resource rather than a definitive guide.

AI tools can also be useful for assessment design. While many educators have to rely on standardized assessment, these high-stakes measures offer a potentially problematic snapshot of a learner's ability on a given day, as these assessments may burden learners with emerging sociolinguistic knowledge and cultural familiarity (Trumbull & Solano-Flores, 2011). In contrast to standardized language assessment, however, many scholars (e.g., Freeman et al., 2021; Menken, 2008) suggest that there is significant value to implementing multiple and varied classroom-based assessment measures that allow students to demonstrate knowledge and competency more accurately. Importantly, classroom-based formative assessments can easily offer data that informs subsequent re-teaching or student readiness to move on to new learning.

For these reasons, educators must dedicate significant time to careful assessment design. In practice, we strive to connect assessment to key principles of language acquisition and learning. Chief among these principles is the importance of repeated and multimodal exposure to language, which facilitates the connection of form to meaning and the developmental shift between short- and long-term memory (Mitchell et al., 2019). In this regard, language acquisition is aligned with general learning mechanisms. Thus, we have found value in prompting AI to generate assessments that intentionally recycle target learning outcomes and linguistic structures. For example, in a course in reading and writing that we teach, we have created low-stakes quizzes from AI-generated stories that utilize vocabulary and themes in previous and current units.

Another learning principle that guides us is the retrieval effect. According to Lang (2016), tests that require students to practice recalling knowledge can in turn enhance students' knowledge. For example, entrance and exit tickets that ask students to recall or summarize learning are a pedagogical tool to reinforce the learning itself and serve as a formative measure. AI tools can support each of these assessment principles as they can save teachers' time in creating traditional assessments such as entrance and exit tickets, multiple-choice quizzes, comprehension or discussion questions, fill-in-the-blank challenges, and writing prompts.

In addition, smart prompt engineering helps create low-stakes retrieval practice opportunities with the intentional interleaving of previously studied language structures, vocabulary, and concepts. Here, we also see AI as a time-saving tool in creating assessments. For example, we have used AI to generate engaging and personalized stories that target specific vocabulary or grammatical structures. Besides being more fun, these also provide context for language instruction and assessment. Rather than simply practicing target language, students are encouraged to think about how grammar and word choice affect meaning more broadly. As additional examples, AI can be useful in generating creative writing prompts, designing project-based assessments, and generating rubrics. By feeding language and/or content standards as well as target learning outcomes from assignment guidelines into prompts to generate rubrics, teachers can confirm that assessments reach broader learning goals. As noted in Table 4, teachers can indeed off-load some of the heavy lifting of traditional assessment design to AI, and it can also help educators design and utilize assessment measures in exciting new ways.

In addition to supporting traditional assessment measures, careful prompting of generative AI chatbots allows us to improve upon measures that better support learning and are more inclusive of diverse ways of showing knowledge. First, it can be easier to ensure that a given assessment supports long-term learning goals via intentional interleaving. Second, AI tools can serve as valuable assistants when it comes to thinking deeply about *washback*. Washback refers to the impact or influence that the testing process has on

Table 4 Augmenting and Re-Envisioning Assessment Approaches with AI

AI for Traditional Assessment Measures	AI-Enhanced Assessment Approaches
AI can be used to generate: • Entrance tickets • Exit tickets • Multiple-choice quizzes • Fill-in-the-blank and cloze exercises • Comprehension and discussion questions • Writing prompts • Project-based assessments • Rubrics	AI can further enhance assessment by: • Interleaving concepts from prior learning and new learning with regularity • Evaluating whether assessments connect to standards and/or language objectives • Building customized rubrics based on proficiency levels and goals • Developing student interest-aligned projects to assess knowledge of specific content and language • Contextualizing syntactical assessment by using target language structures in texts and stories • Ensuring that content assessments utilize familiar vocabulary to reduce linguistic barriers to showing knowledge • Analyzing assessment results for trends to consider reteaching and grouping • Creating adaptive assessments that target mastery before moving forward • Assisting with initial grading of assignments and/or writing feedback

teaching and learning and emphasizes the reciprocal relationship between assessment and instruction, acknowledging that assessments not only measure learning but can also shape teaching and learning. Using AI as a data analysis tool, educators can more easily analyze the results of assessments for trends that allow for data-informed instructional decisions. Considering which communicative scenarios, vocabulary, or language structures most students missed or even what language structures were either used incorrectly or missing from student writing opens a space not only for needed re-teaching or practice but also for purposeful grouping of students.

Third, and quite importantly, AI can support inclusive assessment practices that allow students to share their knowledge via diverse means that more closely align to individual and/or cultural knowledge. For example, while traditional assessments focus on reading and writing, AI makes it easier to generate multimodal assessments that require students to listen and speak. Furthermore, for those who are simultaneously teaching English language alongside content, AI can be prompted to build assessments that utilize familiar vocabulary so that linguistic barriers to showing content knowledge can be minimized. Finally, AI opens a window to creating adaptive assessments that target mastery but also allow learners to flourish at their own pace and according to their own needs. Maximizing AI tools in these ways will require practice and experimentation, but the potential rewards for this effort are significant.

Make It Your Own

Application Activity

A. Explore a formative assessment

1. **Choose a Lesson Plan:** Select a recent lesson for which you would like to develop a formative assessment.
2. **Select an AI-Powered Tool:** Identify an AI-powered tool that is adapted to the type of assessment you are interested in. For example, you may be interested in a tool that can review readings and develop comprehension questions or one that can generate quizzes.

3. **Prepare Your Prompt:** Prompt your selected tool for suggested assessments. Be sure to provide appropriate context, such as age, proficiency level, and learning goals.

4. **Analyze the Output:** Carefully review the AI's output. Reflect on these questions:
   - How well does the assessment align with learning goals?
   - Will this work as a formative assessment? That is, will the results help you consider either areas in need of reteaching or how to organize students going forward?
   - Can you prompt the AI tool to improve the output?

5. **Think outside of the box:** For the same formative assessment, prompt an LLM tool like ChatGPT or Gemini to brainstorm alternative assessment ideas. Consider:
   - strategies to increase authentic interaction
   - giving students agency over how they demonstrate learning

6. **Reflect on the Experience:** Take fifteen minutes to jot down your thoughts on the process. Think about:
   - How might you utilize AI support for regular retrieval practice exercises and formative assessment?
   - Does this use of AI affirm or alter your assessment philosophy? How?

B. Explore a summative assessment

1. **Choose a Unit:** Select a unit or broader learning goal for which you would like to develop a summative assessment.

2. **Select an AI-Powered Tool:** Identify an AI-powered tool that is adapted to the type of assessment you are interested in. While you may use multiple tools in the assessment design process, beginning with a chatbot to brainstorm assessment options is a good idea.

3. **Prepare Your Prompt:** Prompt your selected tool to brainstorm assessments. Be sure to provide appropriate context, such as students' age, proficiency level, and learning goals. You may also want to indicate whether you would like the assessment to include multimodal options for students, such as a writing and a speaking component.

4. **Analyze the Output/Prompt Reiteration:** Carefully review the AI tool's suggestions. Consider:
   - How well did the AI-powered tool align with the learning goals of the selected unit?
   - Did the suggested assessments seem appropriate for the students' age and proficiency level?
   - As you deem appropriate, refine your prompt or ask additional questions to improve upon the assessment suggestions. You may also consider using AI-support to develop assessment directions and/or rubrics.
5. **Reflect on the Experience:** Take fifteen minutes to jot down your thoughts on the process. Think about:
   - Did the tool provide valuable insights for crafting clear and effective assessment instructions and criteria?
   - In what ways did the AI-powered tool enhance the assessment design process?
   - Were there any limitations or challenges in using the tool for brainstorming assessment options?
   - Does this use of AI affirm or alter your assessment philosophy? How?

It is difficult to quantify the potential rewards of AI utilization for educators, as creative prompting can open seemingly limitless avenues in alignment with our own particular needs and teaching philosophies. Nonetheless, we must think comprehensively about AI. Just as we can utilize these tools to save time, our students can too. Indeed, many scholars (e.g., Crompton & Burke, 2024; Eke, 2023; Rudolph et al., 2023) note that in addition to productive supports, AI-powered tools present new challenges to academic integrity that must be addressed. For example, in our practice, we often ask students to annotate readings. AI can now do this for them. We ask them to write summaries or respond to comprehension questions. AI can do this too. We have assigned synthesis writing to find common themes across texts, yet AI can do this as well. With all the ways that AI can outsmart our assessments, how can we still encourage students to engage in the important struggle that learning requires?

Supiano (2023) suggests that assessment should include critical engagement so that just using AI output will not be enough to demonstrate learning. In this vein, Clay (2023) has explored prompting AI with rubrics and exemplars for first-pass efforts at evaluating student writing and then following this up with one-on-one conferences that permit personalized discussion and deeper engagement. We have also had success generating writing assignments with students to critique the output and better understand the assignment goals. For example, we have always asked students to reflect on the writing process after writing multiple drafts, but now this reflection includes questions about if and how AI was helpful to the process. Our students have commented that they appreciate the transparent dialogue, as it destigmatizes the use of AI as a support tool and launches important discussions about writing and feedback.

In addition to using AI to help design assessments, we are also rethinking assessments to be more resistant to AI. For instance, AI can answer written comprehension questions and even design student presentations, but we can now also ask students to answer questions in an interview or in a Q&A session. Building live interaction with peers and teachers into assessments makes assessment an active exercise in expressive and receptive communication. While these approaches are time-consuming rather than time-saving, they offer added advantages of more personalized assessment, stronger classroom relationships, and a renewed focus on language education to connect people. The irony is that the technology pushes us to innovate, yet some of that innovation is a more hands-on approach allowing us "to remember the social nature of education and the consequent importance of teachers" (Liu et al., 2023, para. 1). For the three authors, our connection with students is the most joyful aspect of our work as ELT professionals.

AI in Assignment Design

We have reviewed many ways in which AI can support lesson planning and assessment, but the nature of how we update or create engaging assignments is now open to potential disruption. As with lesson planning and assessment, AI tools can help educators align assignments to broader curricular goals and brainstorm new ways of achieving those goals. However, we often do not need to start from scratch because AI can enhance existing assignments. One approach is to input an existing assignment and ask a chatbot to complete it.

Is your assignment immune, or at least highly resistant, to complete AI generation? Does the output help you think about how your assignment can be made more creative or personalized? Does the output provide an interesting model for your students to evaluate? These are questions we can ask ourselves when experimenting with new AI platforms.

In our own teaching, AI has become useful in fine-tuning our assignment guidelines. In one instance, we enhanced a phased writing assignment that was conducted over several weeks. By inputting the overall learning goals and the desired steps, the AI tool generated a detailed list of steps and directions for students. We then generated rubrics for each phase of the assignment. After a careful review of the output, some prompt refinement, and a few personal adjustments, we made significant revisions to the assignment in very little time.

Similarly, AI can be useful in enhancing our standard assignment practices. For example, AI tools can be prompted to review text, audio, or video alongside learning objectives to brainstorm new assignments. We can also more efficiently personalize assignments based on student interests and course content. By integrating AI into our assignment practices, we can create tailored experiences for students.

Make It Your Own

Application Activity

1. **Choose an Existing Assignment:** Select an existing assignment that you often use or are planning to use.
2. **Open an AI writing assistant:** Text generation platforms like ChatGPT, HuggingChat, or Gemini will work well for this task.
3. **Prepare Your Prompt:** Use the following template to craft a prompt for the AI:
   - "I have an assignment for a group of students [describe age and proficiency level] focusing on [describe the key elements of the assignment, such as topic, objectives, and final product]. Could you complete the assignment?"
4. **Submit Your Prompt:** Enter your prompt as well as the assignment guidelines into the selected AI tool.

5. **Analyze the Output:** Carefully review the AI's output. Reflect on:
   - How well did the AI complete your assignment?
   - Are there ways the assignment should be altered? (That is, can the assignment be altered to include more personal reflection or focus more on the process than on the product?)
   - Can the output be used as a model for students to analyze and discuss?
6. **Input follow-up prompts:** Based on your analysis, consider possible follow-up prompts, such as:
   - "Based on the learning objectives, how might I improve the assignment?"
   - "Generate a rubric for this assignment."
   - "Are there any additional resources or techniques that could enhance this assignment?"
7. **Reflect on the Experience:** Take fifteen minutes to jot down your thoughts on the process. Think about:
   - How did the AI's feedback align with your teaching philosophy and goals?
   - What potential benefits and challenges did you encounter in using this AI tool?
   - How might you integrate AI into your assignment development process in the future?

AI in Curriculum Development

When it comes to curriculum development, AI can be a powerful assistant that can support our efforts to align teaching to developmental standards. By supplying these standards as well as additional details about our students' proficiency levels and the amount of time we have to reach learning goals, AI can be used to map broader learning targets into manageable chunks. Moreover, AI tools can be prompted to ensure we consistently schedule interleaving and retrieval practice to reinforce learning. Surely, we can map curriculum on our own or institutions can purchase them for us. What AI offers us, though, is the ability to efficiently generate a more personalized curriculum. Once we know our students well, we can use AI to adapt existing curricular materials or to generate an entirely new path to learning. As we can customize assignments, lessons, and assessments, we can utilize AI tools to innovate teaching and learning on a much broader scale. For this purpose, consider the current classes of tools available (Table 5) and use the AI evaluation table in Chapter 2.

Furthermore, AI tools can be used to enhance equity and representation in curricula. While paywalls to access enhanced service may expand the digital divide, many AI tools and chatbots have high-quality free versions, allowing educators to engage in highly customized curricular planning for little to no

Table 5 Classes of AI Tools

Large Learning Models (LLMs)/Chatbots
- AI models that have been trained on a massive amount of textual data, which, in response to user queries, can produce human-like language. LLMs can be finetuned for specific applications, responses to questions, text generation, translation, summarization, and much more.

Adaptive Learning Platforms
- Platforms that use AI to assess individual student performance and adapt learning content accordingly. These platforms can provide personalized learning paths based on each student's strengths and weaknesses.

Predictive Analytics/Learning Analytics
- AI-powered tools to gather and analyze data on student performance. These tools offer insight into trends relating to effectiveness of teaching methods and interventions for struggling students.

Automated Grading Systems
- AI-powered tools that can automate or partially automate the evaluation of written responses.

Speech Recognition Tools
- AI-powered technology that can be used to assess language skills, facilitate language learning, and provide feedback on pronunciation and speaking abilities.

Content Creation Tools
- AI tools that can assist teachers in creating and curating educational content, such as quizzes, lesson plans, text, presentations, images, and videos.

Virtual or Augmented Reality
- Tools that can provide immersive learning experiences through simulation

Plagiarism Detection Tools
- Tools that claim to identify inclusion of unauthorized copying of content
- *Note:* These tools often indicate false positives, so they should be used with caution. If you do use them, consider them a tool to teach students about the importance of individual voice in the drafting process rather than to police cheating.

---

cost. Cost savings, however, are not the only way that AI can be a force for equity. Customized curricular design that is generated from the ground up allows teachers and local administrators to build programs that center asset-based representation of the unique cultural and linguistic communities they serve.

In addition to asset-based representation of communities in curricular materials, we see value in using AI to develop inclusive curricula that are intentional about co-creating students' worlds of possibility in a second language. Shardakova and Pavlenko (2004) note that ESL textbooks often "exhibit racial and gender biases, as well as implicit Western middle-class values like consumerism, thrift, delayed gratification, and social mobility" (p. 27). In related work that explored heteronormativity in ELT teaching materials, Gray (2013) found that "LGBT students and teachers were denied recognition and a somewhat skewed picture of world was produced" (p. 56). Thus, we see a pathway to empowering our students by generating customized materials that are both relevant to their lived experiences and challenge hegemonic and normative discourse. Rather than isolating or rendering various intersections of identity invisible, we suggest the use of AI tools to develop curricula that comprehensively normalizes a broad range of identities.

Make It Your Own

Reflection Activity

Consider your existing curriculum or course design. Now imagine engaging with an AI-powered tool to adapt that curriculum.
- How would you like to adapt this curriculum?
  - o Consider how the curriculum could better reflect your students' identities, skills, and goals.
  - o Where do you see opportunities for increased student interaction and/or interleaving?
  - o How could you use AI to explore such adaptations?
- What benefits and challenges do you see to utilizing AI tools to help with this adaptation?

Take fifteen minutes to jot down your thoughts or sketch out a plan for exploring AI support in the area of curriculum design. Reflect on how this exercise might change your approach.

Creating Scaffolded and Authentic Materials

Another exciting area in which AI offers teachers back-end support is creating differentiated and authentic materials. The importance of scaffolded instruction and authentic materials is well documented within the field of ELT, yet there is less recognition of the inherent challenge teachers face in consistently designing materials that allow access to students of varying linguistic proficiency levels. Gottlieb (2016) suggests that ELT professionals should consider both language and content as well as the power of graphics, multisensory inputs, and interactive exercises when designing scaffolds for multilingual students. Indeed, the need for well-designed supports for a variety of students compounds already burdensome time demands on teachers, but there is good news: AI is extraordinary when it comes to generating scaffolds. Table 6 offers a starting list of AI-powered approaches to developing customized supports to varying proficiency levels, but this list is by no means comprehensive. The only real limit here is your creativity.

For instance, we recently worked with a high school MLL teacher in the United States who was struggling to support her students with a mandated curriculum that required reading primary historical sources with antiquated and formal language. Her lower-proficiency students could not access the meaning behind key historical documents, so she utilized an LLM to create new versions of the texts that retained the original meaning but with more contemporary English. Once her students were able to access meaning, she was able to link contemporary vocabulary to the original phrasing, which built a linguistic pathway to essential course content.

We have also found ways to personalize speaking activities via customized dialogues and role-playing exercises that engaged our students in authentic interaction. Prompting AI tools saved us time and enhanced our creative teaching endeavors rather than replacing us or our work. In other examples, we have used AI tools to adapt current news stories of interest to our students to varied language proficiency levels and curated video materials with integrated comprehension questions. In each of these examples, AI tools helped us craft accessible materials that ultimately facilitated richer in-class discussions.

An approach that we often use when designing scaffolds for a diverse group of students is to prioritize planning for students in need of the most support and then remove scaffolds for those who need less support. Philosophically, this may require a shift in how teachers organize their classrooms, like getting comfortable with all students not necessarily reaching for language and

Table 6 AI-Supported Development of Customized Scaffolds

Multimodal Skills	Additional Considerations
Reading	**Translanguaging**
1. Re-create texts at varying proficiency levels 2. Generate texts in home languages (not to be used for pure translation but for metalinguistic analysis) 3. Generate outlines 4. Generate read-alouds 5. Interactive AI tutor that responds to questions via text	1. Generate learning materials (e.g., text, audio, video, subtitles) in multiple languages 2. Create bilingual glossaries 3. Create assessments that allow students to show knowledge with flexible language use 4. Design materials that access diverse cultural backgrounds and histories
Writing	**Visual Supports**
1. Generate models for student analysis and graphic organizers 2. Create writing stems to target particular grammatical structures or organizational features 3. Develop note-taking guides with varying levels of detail to support range of proficiency levels 4. Explore use of AI as a supportive brainstorming and proofreading tool	1. Generate customized video and images 2. Design graphic organizers 3. Generate closed-captioning
Listening/Speaking	**Vocabulary**
1. Generate audio for text 2. Generate sentence stem starters 3. Create dialogues and role-playing exercises that target specific sounds, grammatical structures, and/or vocabulary 4. Interactive AI tutor responds to questions orally 5. Generate scenarios that shift the pragmatic demands of communication (e.g., how linguistic interaction changes based on relationships and levels of formality)	1. Identify target academic vocabulary and idiomatic language from textual or video sources 2. Generate translations and cognate lists 3. Identify language patterns (i.e., similar endings across languages such as -*tion* in English with -*cion* in Spanish) that may be present in readings and materials 4. Generate images of salient vocabulary
	Dynamic Grouping
	1. Generate homogeneous or heterogeneous groups from AI-supported data analysis of formative assessment 2. Use AI to continuously refine groupings based on short- or long-term goals or particular re-teaching needs

content in the same way. However, the potential benefits of this pedagogical shift, in terms of access to content and personalized support to encourage growth, warrant its consideration.

Make It Your Own

Application Activity

1. **Choose an Existing Lesson:** Select an existing lesson that you often use or are planning to use soon.
2. **Open an AI writing assistant:** Text generation platforms like ChatGPT, HuggingChat, or Gemini will work well for this task.
3. **Prepare Your Prompt:** Use the following template to craft a prompt for the AI:
   - "I am conducting a lesson for a group of students [describe age and range of proficiency level] focusing on [describe the key elements of the assignment, such as topic, objectives, and final product]. Could you generate a list of supportive scaffolds for each proficiency level?"
4. **Submit Your Prompt:** Enter your prompt into the selected AI tool.
5. **Analyze the Output/Prompt Refinement:** Analyze the output and consider possible follow-up prompts, such as:
   - "Based on the learning objectives/proficiency levels, what additional vocabulary/sentence starters could be helpful for [describe student level]?"
   - "Refine [describe suggested scaffolds] to include multimodal supports."
   - "Are there any additional resources or techniques that could enhance this lesson?"
6. **Explore other tools:** If some of the suggested scaffolds require visual supports, explore AI image generation tools to create these images. If a suggested scaffold included closed-captioning or adapting varying texts to various levels, explore generating these as well as using whatever tools are necessary.

7. **Reflect on the Experience:** Take fifteen minutes to jot down your thoughts on the process. Think about:
   - Consider any gaps or limitations in the AI-generated scaffolds. How might you address these gaps to ensure comprehensive support for your students?
   - Reflect on your collaboration with the AI tool in the scaffolding process. How did this collaboration enhance your role in lesson planning?
   - How feasible do you find the incorporation of AI-generated scaffolds into your teaching practice?

AI and Instructor Expertise

Although AI tools can surely free up time, they have limitations. Generated materials should always be verified for "accuracy . . . to avoid the possibility of the AI generating creative, yet untrue information" (Bonner et al., 2023, p. 37), and this verification requires content knowledge. However, content knowledge alone is not sufficient to trust output, which should also be analyzed to avoid replicating bias and stereotypes. Furthermore, the decision for how to best implement ideas or materials requires methodological decision-making. Teachers' expertise, both in sound pedagogy and in knowing their students well, will remain essential to implementation of AI-generated materials. Despite the disruption AI has brought to the field of ELT, good pedagogy is still good pedagogy. Teachers need to determine when the use of AI is purposeful and supportive of their broader educational mission. Because AI does not inherently have contextual understanding or emotional intelligence, it is up to us to creatively prompt it and critically evaluate its output. Though iterative prompting—revising prompts based on current outputs versus one's goal output—can create a sense of context, our relationship to students and their experiences remains essential to classroom cultures in which learners thrive. As a colleague in Boston, Massachusetts, reminds us, "It's great to have AI to help with the product, but the process (critical thinking, design thinking) has to be human." AI can support but not replace teachers in ELT.

Make It Your Own

Reflection Activity

In this chapter we have explored many possible back-end uses of AI tools for ELT professionals. However, we acknowledge that integrating these AI tools into one's professional practice can be both exciting and intimidating.

A. With this in mind, take fifteen minutes to write down your thoughts. You might consider:
   - What feelings did you experience when using AI as a supportive tool in material development?
   - How might these concerns be balanced against the opportunities and benefits that AI can bring to language education?
   - How can a balanced view of AI's capabilities and limitations inform your future decisions about incorporating AI into teaching?
   - Reflect on your pedagogical philosophy. In what ways did the use of AI align with or challenge your fundamental beliefs about teaching and learning?
   - How can AI be integrated in a way that enhances rather than conflicts with your established teaching principles?
B. Using the Experiential Model for AI Integration in Chapter 5, experiment with AI resources in one of your lessons.
C. Return to your notes from Part A and reflect on if or how your ideas have been affirmed or changed. Do you have the same view about AI? What surprised you? What might you do differently? If your feelings have remained the same, reflect on why you think your views have remained the same.

Chapter Takeaways

- Rather than undertaking futile efforts to ban or detect AI use, we encourage a willingness to participate and understand an AI-enhanced world.

- AI can support teachers in lesson planning, assessment, materials development, and curriculum design.
- Using AI can save teachers time and provide valuable opportunities for innovation.
- In an increasingly AI-driven world, teacher expertise is more important than ever.

Chapter 4
AI on the Front End: Practical Pedagogical Strategies for ELT

"I've been ChatGPT'd!"
—an English language instructor in the United States

Introduction

If you are in the field of education, you have probably thought about the ramifications of teaching in an AI-rich world, one where many of our go-to assignments can be completed, in part or in whole, using increasingly powerful AI tools. In this chapter we address these concerns by first discussing the need for transparency with students and stakeholders when we deploy AI systems in education. We then discuss how AI can be used to facilitate more accessible and inclusive classroom spaces before concluding with a brief discussion of AI and academic integrity concerns.

Transparency, AI, and the AI-Rich Classroom

We refer to the concept of transparency as the degree to which AI systems can be easily understood by users. One of the ways in which we foster transparency with students is through open discussions about AI and its strengths and limitations. These discussions provide a valuable opportunity to raise students' awareness about AI tools while enhancing their critical thinking skills. For instance, when Rachel and Ilka first began using ChatGPT in the early spring of 2023, they were curious whether students also knew about it and were using it too. They decided to ask students whether they had heard of ChatGPT or had an account and found that the majority of students were using it. To try to meet students where they were, they decided to use ChatGPT for classroom activities and critique its output with students together. Ilka engaged students in an activity in which they would compare ideas they generated about course content (i.e., presentation skills in a graduate listening and speaking course) with ChatGPT output. Similarly, Rachel and her students analyzed generated debate constructives, a process that not only illuminated the shortcomings of the generated output to replace individual perspectives but also deepened the students' understanding of persuasive argumentation. Bringing ChatGPT into the classroom in an explicit way opened the door to class activities, discussion, and shared exploration between instructors and students.

As Hommel and Cohen (2023) noted, opening up space in class for discussions about AI can also minimize students' anxiety and "offers a unique opportunity to model vulnerability, intellectual curiosity, and the willingness to learn alongside our students." Based on our experiences, we have found that discussing generative AI tools openly with students can also build a classroom culture of trust and mutual exploration. As one of our students in the fall noted in an exit ticket survey "Today's class helped me now and understand what are chat GPT's [*sic*] limits. It's nice to use it in class; it can give different perspectives, and new ideas." Table 7 lists additional suggested activities to create transparency around AI use in classrooms. You can begin by trying one or two of these activities before adding them to your teaching tool kit.

The application activity below digs more deeply into one of the items from Table 7. We provide it here as one that you can modify to do with your students in class to target critical thinking and model an important AI habit of mind—critiquing AI outputs—with your learners.

Table 7 Activities to Build Transparency with Classroom AI Use

Focus	Tips	Rationale
Raising awareness of existing institutional policies	Distribute the institutional or program AI policy in class in a jigsaw activity and ask students to "teach" their section to the class	Students may receive this information during orientation and/or the first week of classes when they are overwhelmed, so reviewing it in greater depth is worthwhile
Communicating expectations for AI use	Model your own AI use in developing teaching materials	Students' investment in their work may increase when they understand how and why they are completing an assignment

Focus	Tips	Rationale
Developing classroom guidelines with students	Craft a policy for your particular course with students	Including students in conversations about appropriate AI use involves them in decision-making about policies that impact them
Helping students understand AI systems and building critical thinking skills	Compare and contrast student work with AI-generated work to explore strengths and limitations	Critically analyzing output is a skill students will need if they are to use generative AI tools for schoolwork and beyond
Get student feedback	Ask students to complete an anonymous online survey or exit slip	Students can offer valuable insights into how class activities are going and what could be improved; they can also help teachers understand whether students need additional support.
Ensure that students have access to AI tools	Students can use free versions of AI applications (e.g., Bing Copilot)	Using free tools can prevent barriers to accessibility for students who are interested in experimenting with AI
Provide opportunities for students to read and talk about AI developments	Incorporate readings and news articles about AI into a range of courses (e.g., an audio passage or video interview with AI experts for listening practice in a listening/speaking course)	AI developments continue to evolve rapidly, and remaining up-to-date is essential to digital AI literacy
Support ongoing learning outside of the classroom	Sharing campus resources that center on AI can enhance student learning outside the classroom and reinforce the notion that AI will impact all disciplines beyond language learning	Extending learning outside the classroom reinforces the notion that maintaining critical AI literacy skills is crucial while students are enrolled in school and then beyond

(Continued)

Table 7 (*Continued*)

Focus	Tips	Rationale
Discuss data privacy and data legitimacy	Choose a short reading from a popular press source to read and discuss with students	Students must understand how their data is used by AI systems so they can make good choices about how to use these tools

---

Make It Your Own

Application Activity

AI-Assisted Problem-Solving Activity for ELT Classes

Objective: To enhance students' critical thinking, language skills, and understanding of AI's role in problem-solving.

Materials Needed

- Access to an AI tool capable of suggesting solutions to problems (e.g., an AI language model)
- Problem scenarios relevant to the curriculum or real-world situations
- Whiteboard or digital platform for sharing ideas
- Note-taking materials for students

Activity Steps

1. **Introduction**
   - Briefly explain the concept of AI and its application in problem-solving.
   - Introduce the problem-solving activity and its objectives.
2. **Problem Presentation**
   - Present a well-defined problem to the class. This could be related to a current topic of study or a real-world issue.
   - Divide the class into small groups for discussion.

3. **AI Solution Generation**
   - Demonstrate how to use the AI tool to generate initial solutions or ideas for the presented problem.
   - Allow each group time to interact with the AI tool and write down its suggestions.
4. **Group Discussion and Refinement**
   - In groups, students discuss the AI-generated solutions.
   - Encourage students to critique these solutions, focusing on feasibility, creativity, and relevance.
   - Each group works to refine or develop their own nuanced solutions, inspired by the AI's input but improved with their insights.
5. **Class Presentation and Feedback**
   - Each group presents their solution to the class.
   - Encourage a class-wide discussion, allowing students to give feedback on each other's ideas and compare them with the AI's suggestions.
6. **Reflection and Language Focus**
   - Conclude with a reflective session where students discuss what they learned about AI in problem-solving and how their solutions evolved.
   - Highlight and discuss any interesting language structures or vocabulary used during the activity.

Follow-Up

- Assign a reflective writing task where students describe how they used AI in problem-solving and their views on its effectiveness.
- Plan future sessions where students can tackle different problems, allowing them to see their growth in AI literacy and problem-solving skills over time.

AI for Inclusive and Accessible Classroom Practice

In Chapter 3, we explored how AI can help educators design inclusive and accessible lesson plans and materials, yet the use of AI *in* class *with* learners also offers innovative opportunities for meeting the needs of diverse learners.

The first way in which front-end AI use can foster more inclusive learning in class is through real-time translanguaging support. Translanguaging practices promote an intentional connection between home languages and the English language. By connecting English language learning to existing knowledge in students' home language, teachers can reduce learners' frustration while recognizing and valuing their bilingualism or multilingualism. Furthermore, giving students agency to use AI tools to connect to their home language reinforces the notion that home languages are a valuable resource. This can in turn enhance the visibility and value of multilingualism in educational settings.

AI can support translanguaging and an asset-based recognition of multilingualism by offering real-time multilingual support. For instance, students can utilize AI tools in class for translation assistance to preview content in their home language and then compare it to content in English. This comparison across languages activates prior knowledge, lowers affective filters, and fosters metalinguistic awareness (i.e., the ability to reflect on languages as systems). However, translations alone are not a translanguaging strategy; building connections across languages intentionally is essential to harness the power of translanguaging in language acquisition. Real-time multilingual support can range from seeking vocabulary translations or pronunciation assistance to student-directed questioning for explanations in their home language to enhance content comprehension. In each of these cases, AI tools offer learners agency in their language acquisition process and reinforces home language resources so that English acquisition adds to but does not replace those important resources.

The ways in which learners can use AI in class for multilingual support are similar to the ways that learners of diverse proficiencies can leverage AI to adapt English-language materials. For instance, students can be encouraged to negotiate meaning at varying proficiency levels in myriad ways, such as prompting AI tools to:

- provide definitions, pronunciation, collocations, and sample sentences
- brainstorm topics, which offers possible avenues for content as well as essential vocabulary to discuss lesson content
- generate images to convey their thinking

- provide closed-captioning on recorded videos and video-conferencing platforms
- ask questions about texts or create simplified versions of texts
- ask for alternate explanations
- seek drafting support or writing suggestions
- utilize adaptive learning platforms that target their specific skills and needs

Encouraging students to use AI tools in class in these ways offers the ability to reach for the support they need and demonstrates value for their active participation in classroom activities.

Front-end uses of AI tools can also improve neurodiverse learners' experiences in the classroom. For instance, adaptive learning platforms can adjust content difficulty and pacing based on a student's progress and comprehension. AI tools can also be used by teachers and students in the classroom in real time to accommodate individual student needs in highly customizable ways. For instance, AI can provide supports that help students:

- express ideas with speech-to-text or text-to-speech functionality
- break down assignments and/or course materials into parts
- assist with note-taking
- practice social cues through virtual reality interactions
- parse emotionality in language through text-based sentiment analysis
- consider content via summaries, alternate explanations, and/or immediate feedback

Ultimately, we find that practices which target inclusion and support for multilingual learners and neurodiverse learners support the unique needs of all student populations in a robust way. By thinking specifically about what students need to attain full access to the curriculum and classroom interactions, teachers and students can maximize the benefits of AI.

Make It Your Own

Reflection Activity

This reflective activity is designed to help you introspectively examine your approaches to building an inclusive classroom environment. It encourages you to identify areas where you face challenges, such as understanding neurodiversity or overcoming language barriers, and to consider how AI tools might help you address these challenges.

Activity Steps

1. **Reflect on Current Practices**
   - Reflect on your strategies and methods for fostering an inclusive classroom. Consider how you address the diverse needs and backgrounds of your students.
2. **Identify Challenges**
   - Identify specific challenges you face in creating a more inclusive learning environment. These might include areas like supporting neurodiverse learners, managing multilingual classrooms, or understanding various cultural contexts.
3. **Explore AI Possibilities**
   - Consider how AI tools and resources could help you overcome these challenges. This might involve using AI for personalized learning experiences, language translation, or providing insights into different learning behaviors.
4. **AI Integration Plan**
   - Draft an outline of how you could integrate AI tools into your teaching practice to enhance inclusivity. Think about practical applications and the impact they could have on your students' learning experiences.
5. **Share with a Peer (Optional)**
   - If possible, share and discuss your reflections and plans with colleagues to gain different perspectives and ideas.
6. **Concluding Reflection**
   - Reflect on this activity's impact on your understanding of inclusivity in the classroom and how AI might play a role. Consider setting goals for implementing AI tools in your teaching practice.

Follow-Up

- Maintain a reflective journal on your journey toward creating a more inclusive classroom.
- Regularly review and update your AI integration plan based on your experiences and evolving classroom dynamics.

Application Activity

Empathy-Building with AI Narratives

Objective: To use AI-generated narratives to help teachers and students understand and differentiate between learning issues (like neurodiversity) and language issues (such as ESL challenges), thereby fostering empathy and awareness.

Materials Needed

- AI tool capable of generating narratives or scenarios
- Guidelines on neurodiversity and language learning challenges
- Classroom technology for displaying or distributing narratives

Activity Steps

1. **AI Narrative Generation**
   - Use an AI tool to generate short narratives or scenarios that subtly incorporate elements that show either learning challenges or language barriers.
   - Ensure these narratives reflect diverse situations and characters, encompassing a range of neurodiverse traits and language learning scenarios.
2. **Classroom Reading and Discussion**
   - Share these narratives with the students, either as a group reading session or individually.
   - Facilitate a class discussion on each narrative, focusing on identifying and understanding the challenges faced by the characters.

3. **Identifying Challenges**
   - Guide students to categorize the challenges in each narrative as either related to learning differences or language barriers.
   - Discuss clues and indicators that might help differentiate between the two, such as the main character's behavior, communication style, or interactions with others.
4. **Reflective Analysis**
   - Have students reflect on how the narratives relate to real-world classroom situations. Encourage them to consider how they might support peers facing similar challenges.
5. **Teacher Observation**
   - Throughout the activity, observe students' responses and discussions. Look for insights into their understanding of neurodiversity and language issues.
   - Note any signs of students relating the narratives to their own experiences or those of their peers.
6. **Group Feedback and Insights**
   - Conclude the activity with a feedback session. Discuss as a group how these narratives can help people understand and support classmates with different learning and language needs.
   - Share observations and insights about distinguishing between learning and language issues.

Teacher Reflection

- After the activity, reflect on students' ability to differentiate among the types of challenges.
- Consider how this activity might inform your teaching strategies to better support students with diverse learning needs and language backgrounds.

Follow-Up

- Revisit similar narratives or scenarios periodically to reinforce understanding and awareness.
- Use insights from this activity to adapt teaching methods and provide targeted support where necessary.

I've Been ChatGPT'd! Fostering a Culture of Academic Integrity

When ChatGPT became available for public use, concerns about academic integrity and cheating arose almost immediately. Educators have since questioned whether students would use ChatGPT to write papers for them or answer homework questions; they also worry that extensive reliance on AI tools may erode students' critical thinking skills. As a response, some schools completely banned ChatGPT, as the Department of Education in New York City did in 2023. Other responses have included a rush to develop and implement AI detection programs that can identify AI-produced writing in student work. Despite teachers' best intentions to use generative AI to enhance learning, we cannot deny that students may still use generative AI tools in ways that go against academic integrity policies. For instance, a student who uses ChatGPT to produce a paper and then submits this paper as their own has misrepresented their work. When a student's writing style seems different than an assignment that was previously submitted, their teacher may suspect that the student did not write it themselves. These situations may lead a teacher to declare, "I've been ChatGPT'd!"

For these reasons, it may seem that developments in AI, and GenAI in particular, have brought an entirely new dimension to the "old" problem of academic dishonesty. However, the three of us take a more optimistic view that while AI tools exist today, we can address new tools with old techniques (i.e., teaching practices that already work well). Below we list examples from our teaching that have helped us address GenAI use, particularly in our writing courses. While these examples are not necessarily new, we would argue that they are even more important in an AI-enhanced world.

- Scaffolding writing assignments into smaller and manageable pieces
- Ensuring students understand what they read so they can appropriately refer to outside sources (if applicable)
- Offering individual conferences with students at varying stages of the writing process
- Providing students with opportunities to talk about writing and reflecting on the course
- Discussing what academic integrity means in an AI world
- Offering multiple low-stakes opportunities for students to practice writing skills
- Providing ongoing feedback on multiple stages of student work
- Recasting assignment guidelines for neurodiverse learners

- Helping students to parse instructions
- Providing guidance for students to manage their time in working on assignments

In most cases, we believe that our best course of action is to encourage a *pedagogical* stance toward AI rather than a *punitive* one. Although educational uses of AI are still in their infancy, many of the same practices we have used to foster a culture of academic integrity before GenAI can be leveraged to help students understand how and when to use AI tools. We should aim to build a culture of trust and mutual respect rather than reinforcing an "us versus them" mindset. This allows us to focus more on learning than on detection so that we can better facilitate language learning and build students' critical AI literacy skills.

Similarly, we advise against using AI detection tools, as they often fail to accurately detect AI-enhanced writing. They have also been shown to be biased against second language writers (Myers, 2023) and to produce false positive results (Dalalah & Dalalah, 2023). Using detection tools for punitive purposes can also erode trust between instructors and students, making it difficult for instructors to work with students as co-collaborators. As one of our students noted, "I feel like it should be used as a tool instead of seen as a threat. It does not work for personal, critical thinking responses, but it is a quick way of research and idea organization." Creating space to work alongside students can open up new opportunities for mutual learning and understanding.

Ethical Considerations

Ethical considerations should be deeply embedded into every element of AI integration into teaching (see also Chapter 1). A critical element of using AI ethically is ensuring that students understand how their data is used. For example, if teachers are using AI for first-pass grading or analyzing assessment results, it is important to note if and how their students' data is being stored and/or utilized. Of note, at the time of this publication, OpenAI and Google both use user inputs as sources of future training data in their LLMs. However, constitutional AI systems like Anthropic Claude 2 do not currently maintain inputted data to train future interactions of the system. What is clear is that we need to consider these ethical matters not only as individual educators but also in coordination with school-level policies. Through individual experimentation, collaboration with peers, and discussion with administrators, policies can be established that prioritize data privacy in schools but maximize the benefits of AI.

Students' views on using AI must also be considered. For example, students should never be required to create accounts with AI service providers in order to participate in in-class activities. While we have found that many of our students already have accounts, we give them the option to use an account we have made for in-class work, to join a group where at least one member already has an account, or to use a service like llama2.space that provides model demos without the need to log in to the service. More recently, the ability to run open-source models (e.g., llama2, vicuna 13-B, or mistral 7B) on a local machine with no communication to external servers after initial installation has become more accessible for users. However, the speed and reliability of this solution are problematic as they depend on the power of the user's computer. Said more simply, if the student is working from an underpowered, economically priced device, the output can be as slow as 1.5 tokens (chunks of a word) per second. Meanwhile, a student accessing from a powerful gaming machine with updated CPU and GPU can expect an experience very similar to using web-based AIs like ChatGPT.

Finally, we strongly advise our students not to put any information into GenAI tools that is sensitive and personal (e.g., medical information, financial questions) and could identify them. We discuss the technical limitations and biases inherent to ChatGPT and other tools and model critical analysis of AI output in class activities. We also emphasize the importance of checking the accuracy of output and not simply taking it at face value. Finally, we prioritize collecting student feedback about class activities and on their learning. Examples include asking students to complete anonymous electronic surveys or exit slips at the end of class. Below we list a series of questions to help teachers navigate ethical considerations of AI.

- What policies are currently in place in your school or institution regarding data privacy and AI use?
  - o   Do institutional data policies account for the current AI-enhanced environment?
  - o   How often are they updated? How can teachers be involved in revising these policies?
  - o   How can you make sure that students understand these policies?

- For each tool, look up how it collects and/or uses inputted data?
  - o   Does this use of data align with institutional policy?
  - o   If not, what changes need to be made? (e.g., revision to policy or changed/halted use of the tool)
  - o   Is data being used in any way that would require parent and/or student permissions?
- Is student privacy protected . . .
  - o   . . . by the tool?
  - o   . . . through educator anonymization of assessments and assignments?
- Do institutional data policies account for the AI-enhanced environment? How can they be updated?

Make It Your Own

Application Activity

1. **Select an AI Platform:** Choose an AI platform commonly used in language education. Make sure that it is a tool that you or your institution currently use or are considering for future use.
2. **Access and Review the Data Policy:** Visit the official website or documentation of the selected AI platform. Locate and thoroughly read the platform's data policy, terms of service, and privacy policy. Pay close attention to how user data is collected, stored, and used.
3. **Identify Key Points:** Summarize key points from the data policy. Note any information about the types of data collected (e.g., user inputs, interactions, preferences) and the purposes for which the data is used.
4. **Alignment with Institutional Policy:** Refer to your institution's data privacy policy or guidelines. Analyze how well the AI platform's data policy aligns with your institutional standards. Identify areas of alignment and potential areas of concern.
5. **Critical Reflection:** Reflect on how the AI platform's data policy might impact your use of the tool in language education. Consider whether there are any aspects of the data policy that raise concerns or require further clarification.

6. **Future Use Considerations:** Based on your analysis, determine how the AI platform's data policy might influence your future use of the tool. Consider:
   - Are there specific precautions or adjustments you would make in your use of the tool to align with data-privacy considerations?

Chapter Takeaways

- Transparency is crucial; it involves making expectations for AI use available and clear to students and modeling acceptable use.
- AI for inclusion requires us to uses AI to support diverse learning needs and linguistic practices, making classrooms more accessible and facilitating long-term student success and agency.
- Academic integrity and AI are not about creating new processes or policies; rather, they draw from current robust practices in new ways that still center on student learning and lived experiences.
- Critical AI literacy will be essential for navigating an AI-rich educational landscape and fostering informed engagement with technology.
- Working together reminds us of the power of collaboration with our learners and instructor adaptability in integrating AI into teaching and learning processes.
- As you incorporate AI into teaching, it is crucial to use the right tools and ensure that AI is used ethically.

Chapter 5

The Teacher's Tool Kit: Harnessing AI
for Tomorrow's Learners

"Embrace it and start small. If you aren't sure what to do, start with just some revising or some brainstorming to get going. If you don't want to direct students on it, then do it together in front of the class so that they can see what you do and you talk them through it. It is an extremely useful tool and it isn't going away."

—an ELT practitioner in Dallas, Texas

Introduction

Our aim throughout this book has been to build a robust foundation for English language teachers seeking to understand the nuances of AI, both in terms of risks and rewards, as well as strategies for meaningful and ethical integration into professional practice. Specifically, we have explored:

- the types of AI and their applications to ELT, as well as overcoming challenges to integrating AI into practice (Chapter 1)
- the importance of critical AI literacy for both teachers and learners (Chapter 2)
- back-end strategies for lesson planning, assessment, and material and curriculum development (Chapter 3)
- front-end strategies for leveraging AI with students (Chapter 4)

In this closing chapter, we share a teacher's tool kit for trying out AI tools and a framework for AI integration for immediate use. Next, we consider the rapid pace of advancements in AI and their implications for the future of ELT. We end with practical suggestions for keeping up with these advancements, including a framework for evaluating AI tools, and we offer specific suggestions for support, resources, and effective collaboration.

Teaching Tips for Immediate Use

As teachers in the AI era, we are required to embody the adage that we are "lifelong learners," yet we also recognize that it can be intimidating to start.

We have found the best approach is to start small. Taking an experiential approach is a productive strategy for taking the first step and deepening engagement with AI. For instance, we turn to Kolb and Kolb (2009), who suggest that "[b]y consciously following a recursive cycle of experiencing, reflecting, thinking, and acting, [learners] can increase their learning power" (p. 297). So what can this type of experiential cycle look like in practice? Kolb and Kolb's (2009) experiential model can be adapted to advance your AI journey as follows:

- *Experience*
  - o Enact small action steps that you feel comfortable taking, such as trying a new platform for an activity or lesson plan or brainstorming with an LLM
- *Reflect*
  - o Observe the impact of these steps for yourself and your students and create a tangible record of this reflection via a journal or a set of notes
  - o Align new approaches, techniques, and applications with your teaching philosophy, focusing on what supported learning, engaged students and offered you time savings as well as what did not
- *Think*
  - o Engage critically with your reflection to consider how it informs new action steps. Use your reflection notes to make decisions about how you can pivot.
  - o Consider how your reflection informs new action steps.
  - o Share your reflection with peers and seek other perspectives
- *Determine new action*
  - o Establish a plan for new action steps
  - o Consider adapting previous steps or pivoting in a new direction

As shown in Figure 4, this cyclical process of experimentation and reflection is an approach that has worked well for us and guided ongoing professional learning. Keep in mind, also, that this is not a path that you need to travel alone. As we will discuss later in this chapter, identifying collaborative partners with whom you can exchange reflective observations significantly enhances the power and pleasure of this learning process.

Are you ready to get started? Table 8 summarizes a framework we developed that teachers can use immediately to begin teaching with generative AI and engaging in ongoing professional development. In this table, the first column lists the focus of each step. In column 2, we offer tips for achieving

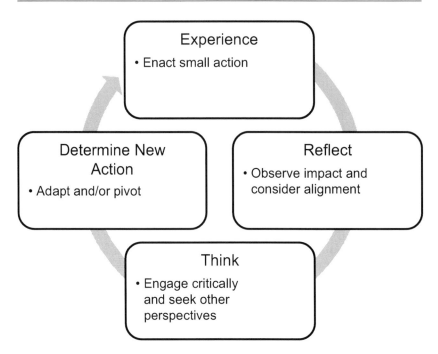

Figure 4 Adapting Kolb et al. (2009) for an Experiential Model for AI Integration

each step, and column 3 provides the rationale supporting each step. While we encourage you to use tips from this framework in the order that aligns with your current AI expertise and/or teaching needs, our first suggestion, to build a professional learning community, is essential for everyone.

The Future of AI in ELT

We have established a productive process for exploring and enacting AI tools in professional practice. Nonetheless, we recognize that many important questions about AI remain open, especially as the field of AI itself continues to rapidly evolve. For example, AI remains largely unregulated around the world despite early conversations and policies such as the AI Act recently established by the European Union (Ryan-Mosley et al., 2024). What policies will eventually govern its use? How will such policies affect training data and our thinking about copyright and intellectual property? Will this change access to AI? Predictions about what is coming in AI range from useful, like supportive systems to help achieve tasks, to frightening, like the proliferation of deepfakes (Lynch, 2023).

Table 8 Teaching and Development Framework for Immediate Use

Getting Started and Supporting Ongoing Professional Learning		
Focus	*Tips*	*Rationale*
Build a professional learning community	• Find colleagues with whom you feel comfortable sharing ideas and collaboratively experimenting. • Establish shared goals and guidelines for communication to support this effort.	Working collaboratively can manage anxiety or apprehension about professional innovation and deepen engagement. We are truly better together!
Stay current with and emerging research in the field	• Attend webinars, workshops, and/or conferences either in person or online. • Subscribe to professional magazines and newsletters. • Follow active peers and associations on LinkedIn or other social media. • Share your experiences and findings with others.	Connecting to a broader community of practice enables ongoing interaction with the most up-to-date research, trends, and pedagogical resources.

Planning, Instruction, and Assessment		
Focus	*Tips*	*Rationale*
Align planning with curriculum	• Ensure that AI activities align with the overall curriculum and actively interleave learning goals over time.	Integrating AI into curriculum planning should enhance learning goals and raise students' awareness of AI tools.
Explore and select appropriate tools	• Choose tools that support customization by proficiency level, incorporate language acquisition theory, and align with your institution's data privacy policy.	Selecting the right tools can create space for you to do the human labor of teaching and meeting the unique needs of your learners, but remember that your philosophy of teaching should drive the selection and implementation of tools.

(Continued)

Table 8 *(Continued)*

Planning, Instruction, and Assessment		
Represent students' multicultural identities and engage in the authentic application of language skills	• Integrate materials and activities that positively reflect student identities and community resources in genuine communicative contexts.	Representation and authenticity can enhance motivation and relevance.
Engage in exploration and open dialogue about AI supports with students	• Implement guided tasks in class to foster deeper understanding of risks and benefits of AI use.	Fostering digital literacy should be a dialogic part of the language classroom.
Prompt students to think critically about AI output	• Design in-class activities that encourage questioning of AI-generated content.	Navigating an AI-influenced world requires skills in critical analysis. Collaboration improves communication skills.
Consider how AI enhancements can assist with both traditional and innovative assessment measures	• Explore AI tools to save time developing assessment measures. • Utilize AI tools to develop new forms of showing knowledge, including allowing students to leverage AI in productive ways during the assessment or project development process.	Teachers can benefit from AI applications to support and demonstrate student learning.
Prioritize the importance of human interaction	• Utilize AI tools to enhance creative interaction among students and not to replace it.	Language is a vehicle for fostering human connection and interpersonal relationships.

What is clear, however, is that changes are already on the horizon. In early 2024, OpenAI created new subscription models targeting teams that explicitly promise privacy protections as subscriber data will not be used in the future (Wiggers, 2024). OpenAI also announced its first university partnership, which will offer unlimited access to students and faculty, the opportunity to customize tutors to university courses, and a guarantee that student data will not be used in subsequent training data (Field, 2024). We imagine that this is the first of many interesting partnerships, yet we worry about the potential for expanding the digital divide for school systems and higher education institutions that do not have similar access to these resources. We also worry about the implications for valuable face-to-face tutoring services that often employ student workers and contingent faculty and offer a social and human connection to students they tutor. Given the evolving regulatory environment and the emergence of collaborations between AI companies and educational institutions, we also wonder how advances in AI will further change how and what we teach in our language classrooms. We suspect that these and many other questions will shape educational debate for the foreseeable future. Staying active in the conversation matters, especially given the speed at which new developments, technologies, and tools emerge.

While discussing the future of AI in ELT feels a bit like looking into a crystal ball, we can make some reasonable guesses about the directions in which new technologies may advance. As we reflect on emerging trends and new tools, we see significant possibilities for both language learning and language learners. For instance, there are new tools that can translate one's voice into another language in real time, and these are already being packaged into consumer devices like the new Samsung Galaxy S24 (Perez, 2024). Before you panic, this does not eliminate the need for language learning or language teachers, as acquiring language is also about deepening new ways of thinking via diverse cultural frameworks. Translation tools alone cannot do this for anyone. We are also noting rapid advancements in video generation, which could allow students to demonstrate knowledge in increasingly creative and personal ways, and virtual reality, which could launch entirely new worlds within which students can connect with others. Furthermore, as it becomes more commonplace for teachers to customize their own GPT tools to support their students and help them reach learning goals, we see endless possibilities for creative and accessible language learning support. We also see here that remaining active in experimentation and classroom-based research allows us to be a part of (re)defining the purpose and means of education more broadly.

In a future that significantly leverages AI technologies, the importance of soft skills through which people interact and connect should also increase. Thus, human interaction and the ability to connect personally and professionally will be more important than ever, which is a realization that is already emerging in industry circles. How are language classroom practices implicated in this future? Purposeful development of soft skills such as teamwork, critical thinking, and meaningful interpersonal communication will remain central to English language teaching. Ironically, AI drives innovation in terms of building students' AI literacy and shaping new approaches to learning while also reinforcing the practices that have always been essential to the English language classroom: interaction and connection.

Keeping Up with Advancements

With frequent advancement in AI capabilities, teachers will need strategies for staying current. It seems that new AI tools are appearing almost daily, and the task of keeping up with these can seem daunting. Stockwell and Wang (2023) remind us that "[t]eachers are humans, and as learners of technology themselves, they need support on a social level as well as a technical level" (p. 479). Attaining both social and technological supports can be done in many ways, and teachers do not need to start from scratch or feel isolated in their efforts to understand ongoing advancements. Many nonprofit educational groups offer regular and easily accessible updates regarding AI tools and integration, and educational materials for teachers, such as LLM prompting guides and online courses, are also helpful. Table 9 lists some of the resources we have found helpful for expanding our own AI repertoires.

For teachers looking to extend their computer science competency, a wealth of free and low-cost options exist. For instance, Codecademy offers free introductory courses to help you focus your efforts and even offers a highly accessible free course on Python, one of the most popular programming languages on the market, in part due to is readability. For readers who need an even deeper dive, freeCodeCamp is an excellent resource that covers a massive number of topics for people from beginner to advanced practitioners in highly accessible and interactive formats; at present, it is free with an option to donate. Joshua has completed a few freeCodeCamp tutorials and found them a good supplement for what he learned in his computer sciences courses—all presented in a manner that is accessible for someone who still identifies as a qualitative social sciences and humanities scholar. If the idea of looking at lines of code worries you, more low-code and no-code solutions are appearing online, and courses that are free or low-cost are emerging, such as the Microsoft AI Builder course on the Microsoft Skill Builder platform or the free tutorials on Oracle Apex. For readers working with young learners, Apple's Education Community offers valuable resources and age-appropriate apps that can help non-technical educators acquire technical proficiency

Table 9 Sources for Professional Development

Organizations Offering Training and Resources

AI for Education
- organization that partners with schools and teachers worldwide
- offers prompt library, curriculum, webinars, and a free subscription newsletter

AiEDU
- nonprofit organization that seeks to empower educators to enhance equity via digital literacy
- offers educator and learner materials, professional learning tools, lesson plans and activities, and a free newsletter

International Society for Technology in Education
- membership-based organization
- offers professional learning via libraries, conferences, webinars, and journals

TESOL
- international membership-based organization for English language teachers
- offers research-based journals, AI webinars and events, and special interest groups

AI101 for Teachers
- a collaboration by Code.org, ETS, ISTE, and Khan Academy
- offers free online video courses, curriculum, and tools

Code.org
- nonprofit focused on educational innovation via teaching computer science and digital literacy
- offers lesson plans and a professional learning community

RAISE
- nonprofit organization run by the Massachusetts Institute of Technology, focusing on responsible AI use for education
- offers AI literacy units and professional development for educators

Cambridge English
- organization that offers English-language qualifications for learners and teachers
- offers a free online learning series called "AI in English Language Learning"

Digital Futures Institute
- an interdisciplinary hub organized by the Teachers College at Columbia University for research-based innovation with digital technology
- offers articles, interviews with teachers using AI, and other resources

---

(Continued)

Table 9 *(Continued)*

Organizations Offering Training and Resources

Stanford University Classroom-Ready Resources About AI For Teaching (CRAFT)
• a resource provided by the Graduate School of Education at Stanford that offers
teaching resources (e.g., lesson plans, worksheets)

Prompting Guides

• *The Beginner's Guide to LLM Prompting* by Haystack
• *Effective Prompts for AI* by the Massachusetts Institute of Technology
• *Prompt Engineering Guide* by the Distributed AI Research Institute
• *Prompt Engineering* by OpenAI

Education-Specific Prompting Guides:

• *AI for Education GenAI Chatbot Prompt Library for Educators*
• *University of Sydney Prompt Engineering for Educators – Making Generative AI Work for You*

Groups to watch for ongoing guidance

Organization	*Recent Publications*
United States Department of Education Office of Educational Technology	*Artificial Intelligence and the Future of Teaching and Learning: Insights and Recommendations*
UNESCO	*Guidance for Generative AI in Education and Research Artificial Intelligence and the Futures of Learning*
Council of Europe	*Artificial Intelligence and Education: A Critical View Through the Lens of Human Rights, Democracy, and the Rule of Law*
Asia-Europe Foundation	*Asian and European Teachers' Perspectives on AI and Education*

through their Swift Playgrounds platform, complete with candy-colored worlds and adorable monsters acting as tutors.

Another important strategy for keeping up with advancements is engaging in conversations with peers. These dialogues can be done face-to-face with colleagues and with broader professional networks at workshops, webinars, or conferences. Connecting with global ELT peers through online professional networks (e.g., via LinkedIn or professional associations such as the TESOL International Association) allows for easy idea exchange and networking. We suggest leveraging these networks to expand your professional learning community, share your own experiences, and benefit from the research of global peers.

In closing, keep in mind that exploring new advancements does not mean that you need to adopt every tool you find. Like any new pedagogical or curricular trend, you should evaluate the usefulness of new AI features and tools in alignment with your teaching philosophy and your students' needs and interests. That said, the AI landscape may also require us to explore innovation *within* our philosophies, including now adding digital literacy to our target learning outcomes. With this exploratory stance in mind, you may also find new ways to utilize AI to facilitate your own learning. In our practices, we have found this critical yet open-minded stance has led us to productive new learning and partnerships.

Make It Your Own

Reflection Activity

1. On a piece of paper, create a mind map that explores your feelings about the pace of AI advancements in ELT. Explore how you feel about any potential challenges you perceive in keeping up with the changes.
2. Using a different color pen, brainstorm one or two strategies to address each opportunity and challenge.
3. Share your mind map with a colleague. Discuss similarities, differences, and approaches for supporting each other.

An Evaluative Framework for AI Tools in ELT

Technological advancements have historically led to changes in classroom practices and in how students engage with learning English. The recent emergence of powerful generative AI tools marks another transformative moment. These tools, characterized by both contributions and threats to learning, also present a myriad of considerations in terms of selection, integration, and application. Given the diverse landscape of available AI tools, educators and institutions face the challenge of discerning which tools will best fit with their curricular and instructional needs and which tools will best support student learning and success. Addressing this challenge is not merely about adopting the latest technology; instead, it is about ensuring that these tools align with pedagogical goals, are adaptable to varied educational settings, and uphold the standards of quality language education in keeping with disciplinary best practices. Admittedly, there is little in the literature to guide decision-making when it comes to AI, although the field of ed tech does provide some initial guidance from which we pull our inspiration for proposed framework (e.g., Attaran & VanLaar, 2001; Banoğlu & Gümüş, 2022).

To address this challenge, the subsequent framework (Table 10) has been carefully crafted to help ELT practitioners navigate an increasingly AI-rich professional landscape. Its purpose is twofold: to provide a structured approach for evaluating AI tools and to serve as a guide for informed decision-making. Although provided to the reader as a checklist, our goal is for this framework to function not just a checklist but as a reflection of the multi-faceted considerations that come into play when integrating technology into ELT. The rationale behind its inception is the need for a comprehensive tool that encapsulates both the technical and pedagogical aspects of AI tool selection. By utilizing and, where needed, adapting, this framework, educators and institutions can navigate the complexities of the AI landscape in ELT with clarity, confidence, and a commitment to excellence. Our framework here is comprised of ten key elements we feel will best aid educators and administrators in their decision-making: Purpose and Alignment, Ease of Integration, User-friendliness, Feedback Mechanism, Cultural Sensitivity, Data Privacy and Security, Customizability, Cost and Accessibility, Research and Reviews, and Scalability. Below, we explain each of these items in turn and how they can be used to help practitioners evaluate AI tools.

The evaluation tool (Table 10) is structured as a checklist, designed to assess AI tools against a set of predefined criteria. Each criterion is accompanied by a series of reflective questions that serve as prompts to guide the evaluator's assessment. For each criterion, the evaluator is required to indicate, based on their judgment, whether the AI tool meets the specific criterion (Yes) or not (No). We provide a summary of each category in the evaluation tool below.

- **Purpose and Alignment:** This criterion assesses whether the AI tool aligns with the educator's instructional goals. It prompts educators to reflect on the specific outcomes they aim to achieve with the tool, how the tool compares to other methods they've used, and its versatility in serving multiple instructional purposes.
- **Ease of Integration:** Here the focus is on the tool's compatibility with existing curricula. Considerations include disruptions the tool might cause, the effort required for its integration, and the availability of resources or support for this process.

Table 10 AI Tool Evaluation Checklist

Instructions: Evaluate the AI tool in question against each of the following criteria. Reflect on the questions provided to help guide your assessment. Check the box if you believe the tool meets the criterion based on your understanding and judgment.

Evaluation Item *Reflective Questions*	Yes	No	Notes

Purpose and Alignment

Does the AI tool align with my instructional goals?

(e.g., vocabulary acquisition, grammar correction, pronunciation practice, conversation simulation)

- *What specific outcomes do I hope to achieve with this tool?*
- *How does this tool differ from other methods or tools I've used?*
- *Is the tool versatile enough to serve multiple instructional purposes?*

Ease of Integration

Can I incorporate the tool into my existing curriculum without major disruptions?

- *How much time and effort will it take to integrate this tool?*
- *Will I need to make significant changes to my lessons or syllabus?*
- *Are there resources or support available to help with integration?*

User-friendliness

Is the tool intuitive for both me and my students?

- *How steep is the learning curve for this tool?*
- *Are there available tutorials or guides?*
- *How do my students react to the interface and usability?*

(Continued)

Table 10 *(Continued)*

Feedback Mechanism
Does the tool offer immediate and constructive feedback to students?

• *How specific and actionable is the feedback provided by the tool?*
• *Can students use this feedback independently to make improvements?*
• *Does the feedback cater to different learning styles and preferences?*

Cultural Sensitivity
Does the tool respect diverse cultural backgrounds and nuances?

• *Are there options to adapt content or examples to be culturally relevant?*
• *Does the tool avoid potential cultural biases or stereotypes?*
• *How does the tool handle nondominant dialects or variations of English? (e.g., Indian English, Sri Lankan English, Nigerian English)*

Data Privacy and Security
Will the tool protect my students' data and not misuse it?

• *Does the tool provide clarity on data storage, sharing, and deletion?*
• *How does the company respond to concerns or inquiries about data privacy?*
• *Are there options for students to use the tool without sharing personal or sensitive data?*

Customizability
Can I adapt the tool to cater to specific student needs or classroom scenarios?

• *How flexible is the tool in terms of content, pace, and delivery?*
• *Are there options to add or modify content based on classroom requirements?*
• *How does the tool cater to students with special needs or learning preferences?*

Cost and Accessibility

Is the tool affordable and easily accessible on
various devices?

- *What is the total cost of ownership, considering
  potential additional fees or requirements?*
- *Does the tool require high-end devices or fast
  internet connectivity?*
- *Are there discounts, grants, or special offers
  available for educators?*

Research and Reviews

Is there solid evidence or positive reviews suggesting the tool's effectiveness?

- *Are there published studies or papers that
  validate the tool's claims?*
- *What are other educators or institutions saying
  about the tool?*
- *Are there any known issues or limitations
  highlighted by users?*

Scalability

Can the tool handle both individual sessions
and larger classroom settings?

- *How does the tool perform with large numbers of
  simultaneous users?*
- *Are there options to manage or monitor multiple
  student accounts easily?*
- *How adaptable is the tool if I want to expand or
  change its use in the future?*

Advice on Data Privacy and Security

To ensure the AI tool respects data privacy:
- Check the company's privacy policy. It should be transparent about how data is used
  and stored.
- Look for certifications or affiliations with recognized data protection organizations.
- Seek user reviews or forums where any data breaches or concerns might be
  discussed.
- Check if the tool offers options to opt out of data collection or sharing.

(Continued)

Table 10 (*Continued*)

Evaluation Scale (number of "Yes" answers):

- *8–10*: This tool is a great fit for your needs and classroom context. It aligns well with most of your instructional goals and other considerations.
- *5–7*: This tool is a good fit but may require some adjustments or additional support. It meets several of your criteria, but there might be areas where it falls short.
- *0–4*: You might want to rethink using this tool. It seems to have significant gaps in meeting your instructional needs or other important criteria. It's worth considering other options or reevaluating the importance of the criteria it does not meet.

- **User-friendliness:** This criterion evaluates the tool's intuitiveness for both educators and students. It prompts reflection on the learning curve associated with the tool, the availability of tutorials, and student reactions to its interface.
- **Feedback Mechanism:** A crucial aspect for any educational tool, this criterion assesses the quality and immediacy of feedback the tool provides to students. It also considers the specificity of the feedback and its adaptability to different learning styles.
- **Cultural Sensitivity:** Given the global nature of ELT, this criterion evaluates the tool's respect for diverse cultural backgrounds, its adaptability in presenting culturally relevant content, and its handling of various English dialects.
- **Data Privacy and Security:** In today's digital age, data privacy is paramount. This criterion prompts educators to consider how the tool handles student data, its transparency regarding data practices, and the options it provides for data protection.
- **Customizability:** This assesses the tool's adaptability to cater to specific student needs or classroom scenarios, its flexibility in content delivery, and its provisions for students with special needs.
- **Cost and Accessibility:** A practical consideration, this criterion evaluates the tool's affordability, its accessibility across devices, and any additional costs associated with its use.
- **Research and Reviews:** This criterion prompts educators to seek evidence of the tool's effectiveness, either through academic research or user reviews.
- **Scalability:** Lastly, this criterion assesses the tool's performance across different settings, its adaptability for future expansion, and its provisions for managing multiple student accounts.

Considering the nature of AI tools, data privacy and security are of paramount importance. To check whether an AI tool upholds the highest standards of data protection, we recommend several measures. First, educators should carefully review the company's privacy policy, ensuring that it provides unequivocal transparency regarding data usage and storage protocols. Additionally, it is important to identify any certifications or affiliations the tool might have with established data protection organizations, as these often signify adherence to rigorous data security standards. Furthermore, users are advised to explore user reviews or dedicated forums, seeking insights into any past data breaches or related concerns. Lastly, it is essential to determine if the tool provides users with the autonomy to opt out of specific data collection or sharing practices, further bolstering individual data rights and security.

The AI Tool Evaluation Checklist employs a tiered evaluation scale to provide educators with a concise assessment of a tool's suitability for their specific teaching contexts. A tool that meets between 8 to 10 criteria is deemed an excellent fit, indicating strong alignment with most instructional goals and broader educational considerations. If a tool satisfies 5 to 7 criteria, it is considered a good fit, though it may necessitate certain modifications or supplementary support to address areas of misalignment. However, tools that meet only 0 to 4 criteria warrant careful reconsideration. Such tools may exhibit substantial discrepancies in fulfilling instructional needs or other pivotal criteria, which should prompt educators to explore alternative options or reassess the significance of unmet criteria.

Make It Your Own: Evaluating AI Tools

Reflection Activity: AI, ELT, and My Practice

Reflect on an AI-powered tool you have used or are considering using in your teaching context.

- What motivated you to explore this tool? What outcomes did you hope it would achieve?
- What benefits or limitations did you experience with the tool?
- How well did it align with your instructional goals and philosophy?
- What unresolved questions do you still have about effectively leveraging this tool?

Application Activity: Evaluate an AI Tool

1. Select an AI-powered tool you use or are considering using for language teaching. This could be a chatbot, tutoring system, or an adaptive learning platform (ChatGPT-3.5/4, Mistral AI, Gamma App, Duolingo, Knewton, etc.).
2. Use the AI Tool Evaluation Checklist to assess how well the tool meets the provided criteria. Carefully go through each criterion and reflect on the corresponding questions.
3. For each criterion, check "Yes" if you believe the tool satisfies it or "No" if you feel there are deficiencies. Make notes of any concerns or areas needing clarification.
4. Use the evaluation scale to determine if the tool is a good fit for your needs.
5. Based on the results, consider any adjustments that are needed to effectively integrate this tool into your teaching context. Are there specific considerations around data privacy, customization, user experience, or other areas that require attention?

After completing the evaluative process, reflect on key takeaways and action steps for leveraging this tool to enrich learning for your students. Consider sharing your evaluation with colleagues to foster discussions about AI integration.

Support and Resources

The emergence of AI into public consciousness in 2022 served as a significant disruption to those working in educational contexts. Supiano (2023) noted that educators were all still recovering from the pandemic-induced changes to professional practice when ChatGPT was introduced to the public. As Supiano (2023) wrote, "What fresh new hell was this?" (para. 2) when referring to what many educators felt with the arrival of ChatGPT. All kidding aside, we appreciate that managing all the change surrounding AI ushers in can be daunting. Lo (2023) notes, "Anxiety stemming from concerns over becoming outdated or replaced, fears over potential misuse of data and a sense of overwhelm at the complexity of new technologies fuel resistance and can create psychological barriers to acceptance" (para. 7).

To prevent or overcome such barriers, we suggest establishing or rein-forcing a range of support. On an individual level, teachers can begin by des-ignating small and realistic action steps in the experiential process outlined at the outset of this chapter. Essential to this process is identifying trusted peers with whom they can engage. Professional collaboration allows edu-cators to share knowledge, deepen their engagement in learning, and feel supported as they navigate ongoing change. We have personally and pro-fessionally benefited from partnership in myriad ways, such as collaborative brainstorming and lesson planning, shared reflection journals, and class-room observations. One factor that we have found to be essential to these partnerships is establishing psychological safety and trust, which grants us more freedom to be vulnerable in the learning process. Arguably, teachers may feel pressure to already know everything, so trusting relationships open a productive space in which we can develop new knowledge. Based on our experience, we suggest the following approach to collaboration for AI-related teaching initiatives:

- **Identify peers who are interested in collaboration.** Having the same AI skill level is not as important as the desire to work together. We can all learn from each other, and the more diverse the array of professional skills in a group, the better!
- **Establish a communication routine.** Set aside some time for collaboration and agree upon how and when you will meet to reflect and exchange ideas, observations, and experiences. Be specific about how you want to give and receive feedback to establish a sense of psychological safety.
- **Walk the walk**. Do the things you encourage your students to do, especially being open to missteps. We often tell our students that we learn when we get things right but learn more when we don't!
- **Go public.** Share your collaborative findings, including successes, struggles, and lessons learned, with professional networks. Collaboration should not be limited to the colleagues working within your school. It is amazing how many supportive new peers you can find out there!
- **Collect data and share your research.** Conduct classroom-based (action) research with your colleagues and publish your findings. We are navigating new terrain, and we will need extensive research to inform innovations in teaching and learning.

While these kinds of collaborations are valuable, institutional support is also required. Thus, we suggest that educational leaders foster what Lo (2023) refers to as a "culture of experimentation" (para. 19), creating a safe space for educators to explore AI. For instance, educational leaders can positively support AI innovation by scheduling time for co-planning and discussion, offering AI subscriptions, funding professional development and conferences, and, most important, listening to teachers' needs and concerns (see also Paiz, 2024). Involving teachers in decision-making and strategy regarding AI will support innovation and cultivate a positive work climate as change is implemented.

While we certainly encourage educational administrators to include teachers in these important conversations, we do also recognize that in some cases teachers themselves may need to advocate for their and their students' AI access needs. In these instances, we see that teachers' practical insight can be valuable to promoting tech equity by assuring that teachers and students alike have access to the tools they need.

Make It Your Own

Application Activities

A. Develop a personal learning community around AI exploration and skill development. Use these steps:
   1. **Self-Reflection:** Take some time to reflect on your own AI skills, interests, and areas for growth. Identify specific AI-related topics or skills you would like to explore or improve upon.
   2. **Identify Peers:** Reach out to colleagues who share an interest in AI, regardless of their current skill level. The focus is on the willingness to collaborate and learn together. Create a list of potential peers and reach out to them.
   3. **Setting Goals:** Develop a plan for your personal learning community. Outline specific goals, such as mastering certain AI applications, understanding ethical considerations, or incorporating AI into lesson plans.

4. **Communication Routine:** Establish a regular communication routine with your identified peers. Decide on the frequency and mode of communication (e.g., weekly virtual meetings, shared online platform). Clearly define how you will exchange ideas, observations, and experiences.

5. **Psychological Safety:** Discuss and agree on how to create a sense of psychological safety within the group. Encourage open communication, sharing of challenges, and learning from mistakes.

B. Establish or expand your professional online presence (e.g., LinkedIn). Identify three new organizations or individuals (e.g., nonprofits, researchers you like) that you can follow for new ideas about the AI discussion.

Chapter Takeaways

- Take an experiential approach to exploring AI integration in English language teaching and learning.
- Begin AI integration with feasible action steps that align with your pedagogical needs and comfort level, and establish supportive professional learning communities.
- AI will continue advancing, but many free resources can help teachers stay in lockstep with these advancements.
- AI tools should be carefully evaluated to ensure that they serve pedagogical purposes and align with data protection requirements.
- Professional collaboration and classroom-based action research can be cornerstones of your AI integration efforts.

REFERENCES

Albanesi, S., Dias da Silva, A., Jimeno, J. F., Lamo, A., & Wabitsch, A. (2023). Reports of AI ending human labour may be greatly exaggerated. *European Central Bank*, Bulletin 113, EUROSYSTEM.

Anderson, J. R., Corbett, A. T., Koedinger, K. R., & Pelletier, R. (1995). Cognitive tutors: Lessons learned. *Journal of Learning Sciences, 4*(2), 167–207. https://doi.org/10.1207/s15327809jls0402_2.

Attaran, M., & VanLaar, I. (2001). Managing the use of school technology: An eight step guide for administrators. *Journal of Management Development, 20*(5), 393–401.

Banoğlu, K., & Gümüş, S. (2022). Supporting technology integration in schools. In J. Glanz (Ed.), *Managing Today's Schools: New Skills for School Leaders in the 21st Century* (pp. 37–50). Rowman & Littlefield.

Bonner, E., Lege, R., & Frazier, E. (2023). Large language model-based artificial intelligence in the language classroom: Practical ideas for teaching. *Teaching English with Technology, 23*(1), 23–41. https://doi.org/10.56297/BKAM1691/WIEO1749.

Brandt, D. (1998). Sponsors of literacy. *College Composition and Communication, 49*(2), 165–185.

Brooks-Young, S. (2016). *ISTE standards for students: A practical guide for learning with technology.* ISTE.

Bybee, R. W. (2000). Achieving technological literacy: A national imperative. *Technology and Engineering Teacher, 60*(1), 23.

Cain, W. (2023). Prompting change: Exploring prompt engineering in large language model AI and its potential to transform education. *TechTrends.* https://doi.org/10.1007/s11528-023-00896-0.

Castro, M., and Gottlieb, M. (2021). Multiliteracies: A glimpse into language arts bilingual classrooms. *WIDA Focus Bulletin.* Wisconsin Center for Education Research.

CHM. (2023). *Timeline of Computer History.* Computer History Museum. https://www.computerhistory.org/timeline/computers/.

Christian, B. (2021). *The alignment problem: Machine learning and human values.* W. W. Norton & Company.

Clay, G. (2023). Oral exams and first-pass grading with ChatGPT. *AutomatEd: Teaching Better with Tech.* November 27. http://tinyurl.com/b8d2by82.

Crompton, H., & Burke, D. (2024). The educational affordances and challenges of ChatGPT: State of the field. *TechTrends, 68,* 380–392. https://doi.org/10.1007/s11528-024-00939-0.

Crossley, S. A., Varner, L. K., Roscoe, R. D., & McNamara, D. S. (2013). Using automated indices of cohesion to evaluate an intelligent tutoring system and an automated writing evaluation system. In *Artificial Intelligence in Education: 16th International Conference, AIED 2013, Memphis, TN, USA, July 9–13, 2013. Proceedings 16* (pp. 269–278). Springer Berlin Heidelberg.

Cuban, L. (1993). Computers meet classroom: Classroom wins. *Teachers College Record, 95*(2), 185–210.

Cukurova, M., Miao, X., & Brooker, R. (2023). Adoption of artificial intelligence in schools: Unveiling factors influencing teachers' engagement. *International Conference on Artificial Intelligence in Education.* https://arxiv.org/ftp/arxiv/papers/2304/2304.00903.pdf.

Curran, M. B., & Ribble, M. (2017). P–20 model of digital citizenship. *New Directions for Student Leadership, 2017*(153), 35–46.

Davies, R. S. (2011). Understanding technology literacy: A framework for evaluating educational technology integration. *TechTrends, 55,* 45–52.

Desmarais, M. C., & Baker, R. S. J. (2012). A review of recent advances in learner and skill modeling in intelligent learning environments. *User Modeling and User-adapted Interaction, 22*(1–2), 9–38. https://doi.org/10.1007/s11257-001-9106-8.

Donnelly, A. (2023). Reps. Blunt Rochest & Bucschon introduce bipartisan artificial intelligence literacy bill. U.S. House of Representatives Press Office. https://bluntrochester.house.gov/news/documentsingle.aspx?DocumentID=4062.

Duolingo Team (2023). Introducing Duolingo Max, a learning experience powered by GPT-4. *Duolingo Blog,* March 14. https://blog.duolingo.com/duolingo-max/.

Edyburn, D. L. (2004). Rethinking assistive technology. *Special Education Technology Practice, 5*(4), 16–23.

Eke, D. O. (2023). ChatGPT and the rise of generative AI: Threat to academic integrity? *Journal of Responsible Technology, 13,* 1–4. https://doi.org/10.1016/j.jrt.2023.100060.

Ellingrud, K., Sanghvi, S., Madgavkar, A., Dandona, G. S., Chui, M., White, O., & Hasebe, P. (2023). *Generative AI and the future of work in America.* McKinsey.

Falloon, G. (2020). From digital literacy to digital competence: The teacher digital competency (TDC) framework. *Educational Technology Research and Development, 68,* 2449–2472.

Field, H. (2024). OpenAI announces first partnership with a university. CNBC, January 18. https://www.cnbc.com/2024/01/18/openai-announces-first-partnership-with-a-university.html.

Freeman, D. E., Freeman, Y. S., & Soto, M. (2021). *Between worlds: Second language acquisition in changing times.* 4th ed. Heinemann.

Gottlieb, M. (2016). *Assessing English language learners: Bridges to educational equity.* (2nd Ed.) Corwin.

Gray, J. (2013). LGBT invisibility and heteronormativity in ELT materials. In J. Gray (Ed.), *Critical Perspectives on Language Teaching Materials* (pp. 40–63). Palgrave Macmillan.

Gretter, S., & Yadav, A. (2018). Teaching media and information literacy in the 21st century. In *Encyclopedia of Information Science and Technology, Fourth Edition* (pp. 2292–2302). IGI Global.

Hommel, D., & Cohen, B. (2023). Reducing AI anxiety starts by talking with students. *Faculty Focus.* Retrieved from: https://www.facultyfocus.com/articles/teaching-with-technology-articles/reducing-ai-anxiety-starts-by-talking-with-students/.

Hsu, P. S. (2016). Examining current beliefs, practices and barriers about technology integration: A case study. *TechTrends, 60,* 30–40.

Johnson, D. G., & Verdicchio, M. (2017). AI anxiety. *Journal of the Association of Information Science and Technology, 68*(9), 2267–2270. https://doi.org/10.1002/asi.23867.

Kem, D. (2022). Personalize and adaptive learning: Emerging learning platforms in the era of digital and smart learning. *International Journal of Social Science and Human Research, 5*(2), 385–391. https://10.47191/ijsshr/v5-i1-02.

Kiili, C., Leu, D. J., Utriainen, J., Coiro, J., Kanniainen, L., Tolvanen, A., . . . & Leppänen, P. H. (2018). Reading to learn from online information: Modeling the factor structure. *Journal of Literacy Research, 50*(3), 304–334.

Kolb, A. Y., & Kolb, D. A. (2009). The learning way: Meta-cognitive aspects of experiential learning. *Simulation and Gaming, 40*(3), 297–327. https://doi.org/10.1177/1046878108325713.

Lang, J. (2016). *Small teaching: Everyday lessons from the science of learning.* Jossey-Bass.

Lim, W. M., Gunasekara, A., Pallan, J. L., Pallant, J. I., & Pechenkina, E. (2023). Generative AI and the future of education: Ragnarök or reformation? A paradoxical perspective from management educators. *International Journal of Management Education, 21*(2), 1–13, https://doi.org/10.1016/j.ijme.2023.100790.

Liu, J., Demszky, D., & Hill, H. C. (2023). AI can make education more personal (Yes, really). *Education Week*, August 14. http://tinyurl.com/wx6umk9s.

Lo, L. (2023). Human meets AI: Helping educators navigate their emotions About technological change. *EdSurge*, August 4.

Lynch, S. (2023). What to expect in AI in 2024. Stanford HAI, December 8. http://tinyurl.com/sw88yzkp.

Marsden, S. (2019). Busuu launches AI-powered language learning. *Busuu Blog*, March 6. https://blog.busuu.com/busuu-launches-ai-powered-language-learning/.

Menken, K. (2008). *English learners left behind: Standardized testing as language policy*. Multilingual Matters.

Myers, A. (2023). AI detectors biased against non-native English writers. *Stanford University Human-centered Artificial Intelligence*. Stanford.

Michaud, L. N., & McCoy, K. F. (2000). Supporting intelligent tutoring in CALL by modeling the user's grammar. In *FLAIRS Conference*, May (pp. 50–54).

Mitchell, M. (2020). *Artificial intelligence: A guide for thinking humans*. Pelican Books.

Mitchell, R., Myles, F., & Marsden, E. (2019). *Second language learning theories* (4th ed.). Routledge.

New London Group. (1996). A pedagogy of multiliteracies: Designing social futures. *Harvard Educational Review, 66*(1), 60–92.

O'Neill, R., & Russell, A. M. T. (2019). Stop! Grammar time: University students' perceptions of the automated feedback program Grammarly. *Australasian Journal of Educational Technology, 35*(1), 42–56.

Paiz, J. M. (2024). Droids don't teach, we do: Addressing AI anxiety in language teaching and learning. *FTLMag*. Retrieved from: https://fltmag.com/ai-anxiety/.

Pasquale, F. (2020). *The new laws of robotics: Defending human expertise in the age of AI*. Belknap Press.

Perez, S. (2024). Samsung's latest Galaxy phones offer live translation over phone calls, texts. *TechCrunch*, January 17. https://techcrunch.com/2024/01/17/samsungs-latest-galaxy-phones-offer-live-translation-over-phone-calls-texts/.

Pillay, N., Maharaj, B. T., & van Eeden, G. (2018). AI in engineering and computer science education in preparation for the 4th industrial revolution: A South African perspective. In *2018 World Engineering Education Forum-Global Engineering Deans Council (WEEF-GEDC)* (pp. 1–5). IEEE.

Papert, S. (1987). Information technology and education: Computer criticism vs. technocentric thinking. *Educational Researcher, 16*(1), 22–30.

Pasquale, F. (2020). *The new Laws of Robotics: Defending expertise in the age of AI*. Harvard University Press.

Pelevina, E. (2023). Fostering innovation and creativity: Insights from our AI hackathon. *Babbel Magazine*, April 6. https://www.babbel.com/en/magazine/fostering-innovation-and-creativity-insights-from-our-ai-hackathon.

Pelletier, K., Robert, J., Muscanell, N., McCormack, M., Reeves, J., Arbino, N., Grajek, S., Birdwell, T., Liu, D., Mandernach, J., Moore, A., Porcaro, A., Rutledge, R., & Zimmern, J. (2023). *2023 EDUCAUSE horizon report, teaching and learning edition*. EDUCAUSE. https://library.educause.edu/resources/2023/5/2023-educause-horizon-Report-teaching-and-learning-edition.

Pokrivcakova, S. (2019). Preparing teachers for the application of AI-powered technologies in foreign language teaching. *Journal of Language and Cultural Education, 7*(3), 135–153. https://doi.org/10.2478/jolace-291-0025.

Ray, B. (2013). ESL droids: Teacher training and the Americanization movement, 1919–1924. *Composition Studies, 41*(2), 15–39.

Richardson, K. (2015). *An anthropology of robots and AI: Annihilation anxiety and machines*. Routledge.

Roscoe, R. D., Allen, L. K., Weston, J. L., Crossley, S. A., & McNamara, D. S. (2014). The Writing Pal intelligent tutoring system: Usability testing and development. *Computers and Composition, 34*, 39–59.

Rudolph, J., Tan, S., & Tan, S. (2023). ChatGPT: Bullshit spewer or the end of traditional assessments in higher education? *Journal of Applied Teaching and Learning, 6*(1), 342–362. https://doi.org/10.37074/jalt.2023.6.1.9.

Russel, S., & Norvig, P. (2021). *Artificial intelligence: A modern approach* (4th ed.). *Pearson*.

Ryan-Mosley, T., Heikkilä, M., & Yang, Z. (2024). What's next for AI regulation in 2024? *MIT Technology Review*, January 11. https://www.technologyreview.com/2024/01/05/1086203/whats-next-ai-regulation-2024/.

Selwyn, N. (2022). What should "digital literacy" look like in an age of algorithms and AI? *Parenting for a Digital Future*. https://eprints.lse.ac.uk/116808/1/parenting4digitalfuture_2022_04_06_digital_literacy_and.pdf.

Shardakova, M. & Pavlenko, A. (2004). Identity options in Russian textbooks. *Journal of Language, Identity, and Education, 3*(1), 25–46. https://doi.org/10.1207/s15327701jlie0301_2.

Strauß, S. (2021). "Don't let me be misunderstood": Critical AI literacy for the constructive use of AI technology. *TATuP-Zeitschrift für Technikfolgenabschätzung in Theorie und Praxis/Journal for Technology Assessment in Theory and Practice, 30*(3), 44–49.

Stockwell, G., & Wang, Y. (2023). Exploring the challenges of technology in language teaching in the aftermath of the pandemic. *RELC Journal, 54*(2), 474–482. https://doi.org/10.1177/00336882231168438.

Sullivan, M., Kelly, A. & McLaughlan, P. (2023). ChatGPT in higher education: Considerations for academic integrity and learning. *Journal of Applied Learning and Teaching, 6*(1), 1–10. https://doi.org/10.37074/jalt.2023.6.1.17.

Supiano, B. (2023). Will ChatGPT change how professors assess learning? *Chronicle of Higher Education*, May 4. https://www.chronicle.com/article/will-chatgpt-change-how-professors-assess-learning.

Tafazoli, D., María, E. G., & Abril, C. A. H. (2019). Intelligent language tutoring system: Integrating intelligent computer-assisted language learning into language education. *International Journal of Information and Communication Technology Education (IJICTE), 15*(3), 60–74. https://doi.org/10.4018/ijicte.201907105.

Tenório, K., Olari, V., Chikobava, M., & Romeike, R. (2023). Artificial intelligence literacy research field: A bibliometric analysis from 1989 to 2021. In *Proceedings of the 54th ACM Technical Symposium on Computer Science Education V. 1* (pp. 1083–1089).

Thomas, S., Howard, N. R., & Schaffer, R. (2019). *Closing the Gap: Digital equity strategies for the K-12 classroom*. International Society for Technology in Education.

Trumbull, E., & Solano-Flores, G. (2011). The role of language in assessment. In M. del Rosario Basterra, M., E. Trumbull, & G. Solano-Flores (Eds.), *Cultural validity in assessment: Addressing linguistic and cultural diversity.* (p. 22–45). Routledge.

Trucano, M. (2023). AI and the next digital divide in education. *Brookings*, Washington, D.C.

United Nations Educational, Scientific, and Cultural Organization (UNESCO). (2021). *Recommendation on the Ethics of Artificial Intelligence.* https://unesdoc.unesco.org/ark:/48223/pf0000381133/PDF/381133eng.pdf.multi.page=3.

Valeo, A., & Faez, F. (2013). Career development and professional attrition of novice ESL teachers of adults. *TESL Canada Journal, 31*(1), 1–19.

Watts-Taffe, S., & Truscott, D. M. (2000). Focus on research: Using what we know about language and literacy development for ESL students in the mainstream classroom. *Language Arts, 77*(3), 258–265.

Wijekumar, K. K., Meyer, B. J., & Lei, P. (2013). High-fidelity implementation of web-based intelligent tutoring system improves fourth and fifth graders content area reading comprehension. *Computers and Education, 68*, 366–379.

Wiggers, K. (2024). ChatGPT for teams. *OpenAI*. Retrieved from: https://openai.com/chatgpt/team/.

Windle, J., & Miller, J. (2012). Approaches to teaching low literacy refugee-background students. *Australian Journal of Language and Literacy, 35*(3), 317–333.

Woolf, B. P. (2009). *Building intelligent interactive tutors: Student-centered strategies for revolutionizing e-learning*. Morgan Kaufmann.

Wright, D. (2012). The state of the art in privacy impact assessment. *Computer Law and Security Review, 28*(1), 54–61.

Zerilli, J., Bhatt, U., & Weller, A. (2022). How transparency modulates trust in artificial intelligence. *Patterns, 3* (April), 1–10. https://doi.org/10.1016/j.patter.2022.100455.

Zhong, H., Chang, J., Yang, Z., Wu, T., Arachchige, P. C. M., Pathmabandu, C., & Xue, M. (2023). Copyright protection and accountability of generative AI: attack, watermarking, and attribution. *Companion Proceedings of the ACM Web Conference, 2023*, 94–98.